Joe, Great to see you at CHP.
Congrats on all your great, recent
work. Best,

10.2016

LOSING TO BOEHNER,
WINNING AMERICA
A CAMPAIGN MEMOIR

THOMAS S. POETTER

Losing to Boehner, Winning America

A Campaign Memoir

Thomas S. Poetter

Printed in the United States of America
10 9 8 7 6 5 4 3 2 1
ISBN: 978-1-61740-418-4

Van-Griner Publishing
Cincinnati, Ohio
www.van-griner.com

CEO: Mike Griner
President: Dreis Van Landuyt
Project Manager: Kristi Hone Schwieterman
Customer Care Lead: Julie Reichert

Poetter 418-4 Su16
177479
Copyright © 2017

To family, friends, citizens, campaign staffers, interns, volunteers, donors, voters, readers, I dedicate this book to the following, constantly in process dream of hope:

When all is said and done, love and teamwork are still the most important things in life. I appreciate them as ideas, and as realities, and I appreciate them so much more after 13 months on the campaign trail and for another year or so stewing about the campaign after the fact. What I didn't appreciate at the time, though, is how precious, delicate they are and how difficult they are to feel and experience and cultivate and generate on the trail. So from now on, I pledge to do what I can to work as a supportive team member, to help out, to understand as candidates or campaigns struggle and call on me for help or simply for an ear. And I vow to learn this lesson, take it to heart, and as a result to live this way as a citizen, that is as someone who cares, who is not indifferent, who pays attention. Now I know what I didn't know then: love and teamwork matter, and they are rare things indeed in politics, but certainly they don't have to be. And as always, it starts with me; I can be and do better.

Table of Contents

Election Results

 – Winner of the Election, Ohio's District 8

Year	Democrat	Republican	Other
1932	Thomas B. Fletcher 45,930	Grant E. Mouser, Jr. 41,234	
1934	Thomas B. Fletcher (incumbent): 39,466	Gertrude Jones 36,112	
1936	Thomas B. Fletcher (incumbent): 49,668	Grant E. Mouser, Jr. 42,565	
1938	Thomas B. Fletcher (incumbent): 33,972	Frederick C. Smith 40,772	
1940	Kenneth M. Petri 44,605	Frederick C. Smith (incumbent): 49,218	
1942	Thomas B. Fletcher 22,753	Frederick C. Smith (incumbent): 33,797	
1944	Roy Warren Roof 34,494	Frederick C. Smith (incumbent): 51,253	
1946	John T. Siemon 22,945	Frederick C. Smith (incumbent): 40,755	
1948	Andrew T. Durbin 36,685	Frederick C. Smith (incumbent): 43,929	
1950	W. Dexter Hazen 28,379	Jackson E. Betts 47,761	
1952	Henry P. Drake 34,474	Jackson E. Betts (incumbent): 75,768	
1954	Thomas M. Dowd 30,592	Jackson E. Betts (incumbent): 52,196	
1956	Robert M. Corry 40,716	Jackson E. Betts (incumbent): 70,690	

Year	Democrat	Republican	Other
1958	Virgil M. Gase 39,343	Jackson E. Betts (incumbent): 62,232	
1960	Virgil M. Gase 38,871	Jackson E. Betts (incumbent): 81,373	
1962	Morris Laderman 28,400	Jackson E. Betts (incumbent): 66,458	
1964	Frank B. Bennett 45,445	Jackson E. Betts (incumbent): 73,395	
1966	Frank B. Bennett: 38,787	Jackson E. Betts (incumbent): 78,933	
1968	Marie Baker 40,898	Jackson E. Betts (incumbent): 101,974	
1970		Jackson E. Betts (incumbent): 90,916	
1972	James D. Ruppert 73,344	Walter E. Powell 80,050	
1974	T. Edward Strinko 45,701	Tom Kindness: 51,097	Don Gingerich: 23,616
1976	John W. Griffin 46,424	Tom Kindness (incumbent) 110,775	Joseph F. Payton: 4,158
1978	Luella R. Schroeder 32,493	Tom Kindness (incumbent) 81,156	George Hahn: 3
1980	John W. Griffin 44,162	Tom Kindness (incumbent) 139,590	
1982	John W. Griffin 49,877	Tom Kindness (incumbent) 98,527	
1984	John T. Francis 46,673	Tom Kindness (incumbent) 155,200	
1986	John W. Griffin 46,195	Donald "Buz" Lukens 98,475	
1988	John W. Griffin 49,084	Donald "Buz" Lukens (incumbent) 154,164	

Year	Democrat	Republican	Other
1990	Gregory V. Jolivette 63,584	John Boehner 99,955	
1992	Fred Sennet 62,033	John Boehner (incumbent) 176,362	
1994		John Boehner (incumbent) 148,338	
1996	Jeffrey D. Kitchen 61,515	John Boehner (incumbent) 165,815	William Baker (N) 8,613
1998	John W. Griffin 52,912	John Boehner (incumbent) 127,979	
2000	John G. Parks 66,293	John Boehner (incumbent) 179,756	David R. Shock (L) 3,802
2002	Jeff Hardenbrook 49,444	John Boehner (incumbent) 119,947	
2004	Jeff Hardenbrook 87,769	John Boehner (incumbent) 195,923	
2006	Mort Meier 74,641	John Boehner (incumbent) 132,743	
2008	Nicholas von Stein 74,848	John Boehner (incumbent) 163,586	
2010	Justin Coussoule 65,883	John Boehner (incumbent) 142,731	David Harlow (L) 5,121 James Condit (C) 3,701
2012		John Boehner (incumbent) 246,380	James Condit (C) 1,938
2014	Tom Poetter 51,534	John Boehner (incumbent) 126,539	James Condit (C) 10,257

Map of Ohio's 8th District

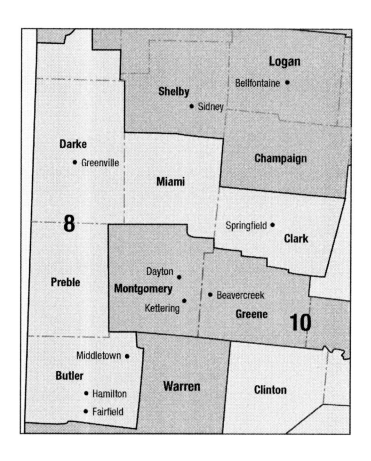

Preface

When John Boehner "retired" from congress in September of 2015 (he actually flat out quit), several friends called me on the phone to ask me how soon I needed to be in Washington to take his place: "Second place general election finisher goes to Washington, right?" I laughed, though flattered, and said, "Second place Democrats don't get a plane ticket to DC." God bless them, they hoped that finishing second in a general election would lead to my filling the seat when vacated. The situation actually scared the hell out of my wife; after hearing the "Boehner quit" news, she called me right away with concern, not hope. I said, "No, honey, we aren't going to DC. This is still our home. No worries. And I'm not running again."

Besides the news about Boehner, not too shocking really, though disappointing, came the quick, official calls from the powers that be for me to enter the race in a special election to fill Boehner's seat and then to run again full bore for the seat in 2016 with Boehner completely out of the way. But honestly, after you read my memoir of the campaign, you'll understand why I couldn't run again, and how high the mountain is for any candidate to climb to establish a working organization that can compete politically on that level against a behemoth like Boehner or any other candidate in a gerrymandered district like Ohio's 8th. We see these challenges play out on the national stage with presidential candidates; the same is true, on a smaller scale, for congressional and other local candidates. But even though I couldn't run again, this book is at least in part about how important it is to run in each race, and how much campaigns give to the populace, maybe even when, or perhaps especially when, the campaign can't be "competitive."

To be honest, what rankles me personally the most after the fact is how all of us left Boehner off the hook for retiring early. He spent many millions of dollars to win the seat in 2014. Then he quit the job he had for 24 years and mortgaged his 13th term just a little more than halfway through it, supposedly throwing himself on his sword to help his party creep farther into the last century. Why should any of us, Republican, Democrat, Independent, or any other, care one bit about the inter-Nicene political problems of a sitting congressman, and Speaker of the House? Why not just give up the Speakership, which he obviously and justifiably felt terrified of losing, and serve your constituents for the remaining 14 months or so, attend meetings, greet supporters and citizens on their turf, and stump for your replacement? These are the things that a noble, established, servant-oriented politician would do.

Instead, the former Speaker left the citizens of Ohio's 8th District with a hefty bill estimated to be in the millions of dollars for a special primary election (held March 15, 2016, to elect representatives from each party to contest for the remaining months of the vacant seat) and a special general election (held June 7, 2016) to fill the remaining months of the lost term! Short of being sick, or just hating the job to sickness, I don't think elected representatives should quit their jobs. It's an affront to citizens. It's an insult to the opposition running hard and nobly on the other side. It's simply selfish.

Obviously, no one cares.

And so we have what we have, a political class that can do almost anything it pleases, and on both sides of the aisle, representatives who remain unthreatened by opposition. And now we have an organized push to the right in uncontested districts that drive the representatives even further to serve a vocal, rabble-rousing minority. That being said, campaigns become even more critical to the public. They are one of the last remaining political events in our nation that give voice and status to the opposition. Campaigns allow citizens to participate in the political process, and to voice their positions and dreams, to enter the fray. It is critical that we nurture candidates, and campaigns in every race. Our lives depend on it. I ran as a "Citizen-candidate," with nothing to lose, and nothing to win. Though, actually, as this work attests, I won so much in the process.

This memoir is about my race, and how difficult, and life-giving it was. And even though I could only run once, I want to encourage other citizens to run, for all kinds of offices. We need good people in all of those political spots, and we need good candidates. Citizens need a choice at the polls, and they need to participate in campaigns.

I also want to say to you before you read this that I have been working hard throughout the process of running and through writing this book, to tell the truth, to surface the pain and joy I experienced, and work toward a resolution of the many conflicts that we encountered. In truth, the hardest part has been forgiveness. I have tried to leave the bitterness I felt and still feel at times behind me, and move on. That's not easy to do. But for me, this is the greatest struggle, in retrospect, and key to making my way forward.

I also don't want to give the impression that I'm some kind of martyr, or a victim. Yes, I felt some things that happened were just wrong, and some things personal. But I got into this with my eyes wide open. It just so happens that high stakes political action makes your eyelids fly open even wider than you could possible believe. I've seen a lot!

Before delving into this tale, it's important to recognize several important people who played a critical role in this process. My wife Chris supported me, and showed her true colors by carrying me through the last months of this campaign. My sons and friends stood by me every step of the way. My campaign staff and interns gave so much. They gave their expertise and their sense of humor and their great effort. They worked so hard. This is something that is impossible to recognize by anyone not on the inside, the effort—the maximum, nearly never sleeping, full blown effort on all of the impossibly time consuming and difficult functions of running a campaign, on a shoestring, and with time running out on us from the very beginning. I also want to thank every volunteer, and every donor, and every voter. I especially recognize the people who gave their time and effort on the campaign trail, calling people and knocking on doors. What a gift. And the people who gave me money knew when they wrote their checks made out to "Poetter for Congress" that we couldn't win, and put the stamp on the envelope anyway. We couldn't have run our campaign without them. And voters, thanks for showing up and checking my name on the ballot. I cherish your commitment.

In the end, several people took time to read advance copies of the manuscript and to comment on, critique this work. Their suggestions improved the book immensely. Thanks to Miami University colleagues Andrew Saultz and Joel Malin, who both followed the campaign intently and who read an early draft quickly and with great skill. Former state representative and congressional candidate from Ohio Pete Crossland read an advance copy, and discussed the work from the perspective of a former candidate. Friend of the campaign and Miami colleague Clyde Brown offered expert insights on the text and the current political milieu. Holli and Dennis Morrish, extraordinary friends, always take an early look at my writing and give excellent feedback. And, of course, my friend Dreis Van Landuyt and his staff, especially project manager extraordinaire, Kristi Hone Scwhieterman, at Van-Griner Publishing made this book possible, in the end. I appreciate Dreis' support and expertise, and for believing in the project, but mainly in me. Thanks to everyone at Van-Griner Publishing for helping get this book in shape and to print.

Last, I want the reader to know that as an educator I hope that this work stands as a testimony to the importance of life experience and the value that it has for shaping our understandings of who we are and what we are to be, what people in my academic field of Curriculum Studies sometimes refer to as the "lived curriculum." We all have a story to tell, and they aren't just random stories; they fit together, and when assembled, they communicate the complicated journeys of our lives. We can learn a lot from these journeys, from these stories. I learned a lot while running for congress, and in retrospect, about the world, and about myself. I hope that my story illuminates what's at stake, and points a way forward for us in some way. It's up to you as a citizen to carry it on, to make sense of it, to live it in your own way. The health, well-being, and vitality of our nation is at stake.

Thomas S. Poetter
Oxford, Ohio
June 2016

Prologue

In *Losing to Boehner, Winning America,* I tell the story of our campaign to upset the Speaker of the House on his home turf, Ohio's District 8 in Southwestern Ohio, in 2014. But I lost to Boehner—a 12-time incumbent and perhaps one of the most recognized members of congress ever—by 40 points. I thought it possible for us to get to 33% of the vote, but we only made it to 27% (a third party candidate got 6%). That still meant that more than 50,000 people voted for me in the general election, and that I got the opportunity to get trounced by Boehner by winning the Democratic federal primary in May. I appreciate all of the people who supported my campaign, and who voted for me in both elections.

I am especially proud that I pounded Boehner in my hometown of Oxford, Ohio, 58% to 42%. Oxford only constitutes 3% of the total vote in the district, but it still means a lot, even though I had trouble with some constituents in my hometown in terms of their sometimes wavering support on the ground and less than impressive financial support throughout. Ultimately, friends and neighbors showed their faith with their votes. Thank you to Oxford's "purple oasis" that gave me that great—though unrecognized—"win" at the polls.

I told my campaign staff from the very earliest stages that I would be writing a memoir about the campaign when it was all over. They joked and laughed with me about it, not really knowing me well enough yet to know that I would actually do it. When my second memoir appeared near the end of the election cycle, in late September of 2014, my life story told through the motif of "Christmastide" entitled *50 Christmases,* they finally got the point that I was serious. It didn't change anything, but my promise to tell our story held up, and here you have my account of our race.

I'm telling my story in part because I want the public to know how important it is to run in every race. Most elections are rigged by money and geography. The public views incumbents negatively, but they rarely lose. It's so difficult to mount a real congressional challenge these days that I don't blame people for not trying. It almost killed me, and I knew that I could never run again. How are people with full time jobs and families supposed to give up two years of their lives to run for office? How can they give up so much of their lives to lose big, especially since the time and know-how necessary to raise enough money to compete lie well beyond the means of most of us?

However, despite the odds and the barriers, which I mostly discovered after I got into the race, I resolved to run as an act of public service. No matter how hard, it's critical that we run in every race on both sides of the aisle. Very few people believe in this, and at the highest levels of Democratic politics, the Democratic Congressional Candidate Committee (DCCC, or the D-Triple-C, or D-Trip) doesn't invest in races like mine that are "unwinnable." This is so stupid, in my opinion. I had to scrape for every last morsel of support from the ground up, with no help from the top. More candidates could run better races if they didn't always have to start from scratch, and that also goes for established politicians running for higher office.

Great citizens, as a result, have no infrastructure to count on if they want to run for office. And when no one runs, many citizens—especially those who feel under-represented long term as the political minority in a district—literally have no one to voice their positions publicly. Running in these races is about building our political and social democracy. We need more discourse, more dialogue, not less. Not running means that we sacrifice so much of who we are. And even more than having no one to vote for at the polls, we don't have anyone to talk to or dream with during the political cycle. Talking and dreaming are at least as important now and in the future as know-how and experience. We need faith and works in politics. If there is no faith, how are we supposed to get anything done, long term, in the remotest of deserts? I have resolved that there has to be a better way! In the last chapter I share several specific, practical ideas for making each race in our nation fairer, and more competitive.

So I try to show how we created a campaign by describing the steps we took. I try to capture the personal drama, the ups and downs from my perspective, of running against the most powerful Republican in the nation. I tell how we built a campaign, how we raised money, and how I ran hard to win but lost. In the process of running, and losing, however, I found out that everyone wins. I hope that some readers will be inspired to participate in the political process as a candidate, or in support of a campaign. Of course, the tension remains that while it's important to run, it's difficult. How can we make it possible for potential candidates to take on the task, maybe even more than once?

This book is a non-fictive rendering of a real campaign—re-created by me after the fact. I do not name most locals or members of my staff or volunteers (most candidates are named). I tell the truth from my perspective. I didn't tape record anything; I produced all of the dialogue from memory. In the end, this is a story with a moral, from my perspective only: You can't win if you don't run, and even if you can't win, you can't lose, either. Running is winning. Let's run, run better, run in every race. Each chapter is 1,000 words or so, to make the book accessible, harder hitting. Here goes.

October 3, 2013

THOSE PESKY TV DRAMAS

I have always loved TV dramas made by the big three networks, all the way back to *Gunsmoke*, then through *The Waltons, Eight Is Enough, Dallas, Hill Street Blues, NYPD Blue, LA Law, Law and Order, ER, Alias, The West Wing, CSI, Without a Trace, Medium*, etc. In adulthood, they gave my wife Chris and me the chance to veg out together at the end of a long day of work, relaxing in bed, watching on "free" TV.

And we have missed shows on other cable channels over the years because they weren't on the big three, like *Breaking Bad* and *Mad Men*, because we never knew when they were on or couldn't find the channel. And when a show got moved to 8 pm, for us it was kiss of death for that show. We had the boys' sports practices/games and baths and bedtimes and such to tend to early in the evening. That's why it was always so hard to watch *24*. And we never taped anything; we could never work the machines right and never had enough discipline to watch the tapes anyway.

Bottom line, I've always admired a story well told, good writing, strong acting, and meaty characters to cheer for and to hate. I love broadcast TV dramas, at 9 or 10 pm.

And so we settled in tonight to watch my all-time favorite, *Parenthood*. From the beginning of the series I felt connected to the characters. Most of the couples in the show were raising children, focusing on issues surrounding home and school. The writers had developed a diverse set of characters and storylines. And I liked the depiction of California culture, the architecture and the topography and the social issues the families confronted. I looked forward to every new episode, a sort of real world escape without the curse of reality TV embodied in shows like *Survivor* or *The Biggest Loser*. While other academics and their students read and prepared for class, I made sure I got my work done plenty early so that I could watch my weeknight serial shows, especially *Parenthood*.

In tonight's episode, Kristina, Adam Braverman's wife, having fought back from her bout with breast cancer, decides to run for Mayor of Berkeley. I thought, "Wow, what a courageous thing to do, and righteous, too." I can remember actually cheering for Kristina when the show ended. She had some political experience going into the race, having helped with the previous campaign of the incumbent mayor. Perhaps she could do what's right, represent citizens, and serve democracy. The idea of running empowered her and her family, on the heels of the "real" fight of her life.

I thought immediately after the show about the current state of our country. When the local NBC News affiliate led its 11 pm show with its take on the ongoing government shut down, in my opinion caused by reckless house and senate Republicans—championed by my own Ohio District 8 U.S. House Representative and Speaker of the House John Boehner— blocking a budget deal in a childish snit over the Affordable Care Act, putting everything we stand for and represent including fairness and integrity and the rule of law at risk, I felt, well, *empowered* by Kristina.

A script began running in my head: "Maybe I should run for congress, knock Boehner off his high horse and out of office. I'm just the person to do it, too. A Democrat, someone with integrity, a fresh face, not spoiled by politics or money or ego."

I knew there were drawbacks. I didn't know the first thing about running for office. But, I had a PhD, how hard could it be?

I didn't have any money for a campaign. Even though Chris and I enjoy strong careers, we didn't have enough dough to mount a winning campaign, even if we thought that was a good way to spend our money. Right, but I could raise it with some effort and a little luck. How much would it take anyway, to mount a reasonably solid campaign with buttons and yard signs with a flashy logo and my name all over them? $5,000? $10,000? $25,000?

Poetter for Congress!

And, ultimately, if Kristina could do it, why couldn't I?

So what if I would be taking on behemoth Boehner?

So what if I knew little about local or regional or national politics?

So what if I didn't have any money, or many friends in politics to call on?

So what if I knew that I couldn't win, no matter what happened?

So what if I based my impetus to run for congress on the storyline of a character in a serial drama series on TV airing Thursdays at 10 pm on NBC starring the former star of *Coach*, Craig T. Nelson?

October 7, 2013
Nuclear Email

In my professional career I have been the victim on occasion of what I call "nuclear email." It usually happens when someone gets upset with you at work and then immediately writes an email trashing you and addresses it to all of your shared superiors; it's a crash and burn scenario. Harm is intended. Everyone gets hurt. I have made a commitment not to send, ever, a damaging email to the crowd targeting someone I'm upset with. And I attempt to shut down the intended negativity immediately if I am the target. If targeted, I shut it down in a short return note and call for a face-to-face meeting. No more email. Everyone knows what a nuclear email is meant to do, and what it does. It's destructive. It's all bad, for the receiver and for the sender, too.

Well, I had never considered the damaging effects of a nuclear email that was meant to do just the *opposite*: not to destroy, but *to give life*. Maybe it's similar to the difference in principle and use between a nuclear warhead meant to destroy a city, country, and/or continent/world, and a nuclear reactor meant to create "clean," sustainable, and usable energy. But maybe the metaphor breaks down because both are bad, perhaps in the end, see Three Mile Island and Chernobyl as evidence, until we figure out how to truly harness nuclear energy safely. At any rate, I got up Monday morning and after having discussed the possibility of running against Boehner only superficially with my wife Chris over the weekend, decided to email a friend with some Democratic party ties in Oxford for some information about running for congress:

Burt, I thought I would be a good candidate for District 8 Democrats to put up against Boehner in '14. Maybe it's too long of a road to take, but I think I could at least stir things up a little. I have no experience and no money. But I can talk, and write. How do I navigate? What steps do I take? Thanks, Tom

Burt wrote back almost immediately, and forwarded the note to a cadre of Democratic operatives in the county, 11 of them. In just a few minutes, the fuse had been lit, and I was running for congress. But I wasn't! I was simply exploring. In my mind, I thought candidates do that, right? They scout out a run, send up a trial balloon, see if anyone thinks it's a good idea, or not. They don't just jump in, even if there is a favorable initial response … Right? Would the party operatives even allow that? Burt wrote:

Hi, Tom—Great! Yes, I think you'd be a great candidate! Your first step would be to sit down with a small group of District 8 Democrats to get you started. When would you be prepared to do that? How about Wednesday afternoon or evening? Once you let me know a time that's good for you, I'll go about inviting prominent area Democrats to meet with you, and we can go from there! OK? Please get back to me as asap.

I just stared at the screen for several moments, examining Burt's response. This was Monday. Have a meeting with party operatives on Wednesday? It can't be that easy: Send an email, someone sends your name around on another email, and you become a prospective nominee for a federal office just like that? Of course, I learned later that it is exactly how it works. It shouldn't work that way, but it does sometimes. Nuclear email. Very quick results. Lots of damage.

The first thing I felt as I stared at the screen was fear. I thought to myself, "Oh crap! Now I've gone and done it. By not laying out clearly what I want to do, that is, get a feel for what is possible, I practically got nominated. I left too much to chance with my open-ended note. I wasn't clear. Now I was reaping what my lack of clarity had sewn."

But I had obviously underestimated the hunger that Democrats had for having someone in place to run against Boehner in Ohio's 8th District. I found out that no Democrat had won the seat since 1939. Boehner had won 12 consecutive terms hands down. I remembered that Democrats put no one up against Boehner in 2012, not even a straw person, even just a name, no one. That's right, unopposed. Unheard of? Maybe not, but exasperatingly embarrassing for a major party. And here was Boehner, still without an opponent only 13 months from the 2014 election while causing absolute havoc for Americans through his destructive tactics, including the government shutdown. Tensions were high.

I was in the right place at the right time. A perfect target.

Over the next several days I spoke with many of the 11 people who got Burt's nuclear email. They were mostly excited that someone with my background would run. Well meaning Democrats in my home county and the source of half the votes in the entire district across all of five counties and parts of one county in the region along the western border of Ohio and along the central corridor of Interstate 70 from Indiana to Springfield, Ohio— urged me on, told me they would help me, sent me information, coached me up. They knew the surface level of my vita: I am a college professor, working in the field of education for more than 25 years. I have a PhD from Indiana University and an M.Div. from Princeton Theological Seminary. I have a stable family and a voting record. I am a published author, with a lifetime of commitment and service to community through my work in schools and universities and as a volunteer.

Tailor made to be fed to the wolves. And the wolves weren't on the outside looking in. They were on the inside of the cage, beginning with the first 11.

A personal Armageddon. The beginning of the end, in an instant.

Nuclear email.

FRIDAY NIGHT
LIGHTS

Our second son Sammy had been the place kicker on the varsity football team at the high school for three years. This, his senior season, had proven to be much more fun and eventful for him. He had labored through an 0–10 season his sophomore year, then a 1–9 junior year, with just a few scores made over those seasons and thus, very few chances to kick extra points, even fewer field goal attempts, just a few onside kicks, and even kickoffs for that matter. But he stuck it out. I was proud of him for that.

Plus he had taken on the punting duties, so he saw a lot of game action, and had actually been fighting through an ankle injury suffered when he got tackled on a botched punt snap that sailed over his head in the second quarter of the team's upset of a regional powerhouse. And each week's game came with great anticipation as the team competed and worked its way back toward a .500 record and perhaps a shot at the state playoffs. The games came fast and furious every week, no matter how the week seemed to slog along with practices and injuries and treatment and such; the games came just the same. Such is life, and as I found out soon enough, such is politics.

As the week progressed toward game night, I went in and out of a personal funk while I tried to make sense of the early emails flowing in and out about running for office. I talked about the idea with some friends, and talked a little bit more with Chris. We had always steered clear of deep political confrontations in our relationship. An Eisenhower Republican, firm on conservative fiscal issues and soft to moderate on most things social, Chris had always tolerated my left leaning streak well enough. But she worried about being besieged by Democrats, or she herself being asked to speak to the issues on my behalf. She didn't want any part of that. And she didn't want to lose any of our money on a campaign. I had to swear that I would spend only money raised, not our own. I swore. Plus she and her family worried about the impact a campaign would have on us as a family unit, and on the boys. What if things got ugly? What if Boehner played dirty politics, making a mountain of some past molehill and ruining us? And a year is not a short time, it's a *long* time. And when Sam went off to college in August, with Mitch already beginning his sophomore year at Miami, I would be campaigning through October, leaving her alone mostly. Also, how would I balance my work, and would the university even grant me permission, per our faculty rules, to even run for office in the first place? Complicated.

I knew I would need support because a congressional campaign wouldn't be easy. So personally, I needed Chris simply to be my wife, and to love me and to care for me no matter. That's what I wanted, and her blessing. That's all. She was willing to do that. I honestly felt that here was no way that Boehner was going to do anything to hurt me unless a poll showed us within 10 points. That wasn't going to happen. Even I knew that, with such little experience, this early. So I brushed off the family concerns. If Chris supported me and I left her mostly out of it, and if I could balance my work and get permission to run from the university's President and not spend a fortune on the race, I thought I could do it. But I still had grave doubts. Was I good enough to run? Did I have what it would take? Could I weather storms that would obviously threaten to overtake me in the 13 month run? Could I ever be as strong and as good as *Parenthood's* Kristina Braverman?

Game night came and I still hadn't decided to run. At tne game, with the team building a sizeable lead at halftime, I wandered over to get popcorn and something to drink at the concession stand. Not many people knew about my impending decision, and I didn't mention any of it to friends I saw in passing and said hello to. Then I saw another old friend and stopped to say hi.

She asked, "So what's new?"

I said, in a moment of intense vulnerability, "I'm thinking about running for congress against Boehner."

Her eyes lit up, "We were just talking at a dinner party the other night about how Boehner does nothing for this district, drags the country down, and we can't put anyone up against him as a challenger. You would be perfect!"

I blushed, surely, and said, "Thanks, that means a lot. But I haven't decided to do it yet. There is so much to consider. Chris is a Republican, I have no experience, and no money. And no Democrat has won the seat in over 70 years."

"That doesn't matter, " she said, "You should do it. My husband and I would support you."

That's when the kernel of an idea to run based on *Parenthood's* Kristina Braverman's inspirational run for mayor of Berkeley became "Poetter for Congress."

I'm convinced that people and events happen for a reason, especially after moments like that one. Of course, this significant, life changing conversation will come back into play later in the campaign. The things people say that are inspiring may inspire, but they may not mean that the person saying them will actually come through for you or actually help you. There is a strain of extreme skepticism in this truth, but also a healthy reality that any politician learns over the course of a campaign involving human beings, institutions, and money.

That night Sam made eight extra point kicks in a 56–14 win, setting a new school record for made PATs in one game. Afterward, with my sister visiting, I told Chris and Vivian that I had decided to run for congress. One big victory leads to another.

October 16, 2013

A New
Campaign

By Monday morning I had gotten the ball rolling on the campaign, carving out a few minutes to put a platform together in lieu of a gathering of the 11 core Democrats from Oxford and vicinity to take place at our home on Wednesday evening. I drafted a letter to our university president and my other superiors Wednesday morning asking for permission to run for office without taking leave. At this point, I would not run if I had to quit my job to do so. I emailed the letter and heard back in just one day that I had the university President's support to run for office. I also invited a few close friends to a meeting at my home, an organizational meeting. A get your feet wet meeting. The meeting that Burt had suggested I have the week before. These were people who I thought would help me with the campaign, at least on first blush.

I wanted to accomplish several things at this organizational meeting. I wanted to see if people in the room thought that I could mount a legitimate campaign. I wanted to test some of my ideas out loud in the room and get some feedback. Was I even in the ballpark, on the right track? And I wanted to hear what people with political experience had to say about next steps. What had to be done? Not just about getting signatures on a petition, but about building a campaign, running it, the big/tiny picture stuff about the political process that I knew so little about going in. Here is the platform I shared:

Platform, Tom Poetter for Congress—"Take the seat, take the gavel!"

- There is gridlock in Washington, but gridlock begins at home. Change will come when new voices enter the fray, making a new way forward for our democratic republic. You can make a difference at home by electing a new representative

- I pledge to represent the citizens and interests of District 8, not those of a small minority caucus.

- I intend on tapping the progressive impulse in District 8, encouraging those without a voice for so long to step forward and take action.

- I promise that I personally will be responsive, open, and transparent in my interactions and relationships with citizens and civic entities in our district, and that I will care about the issues and interests of all of District 8's citizens.

- I pledge to be a learner on this journey, and to provide leadership.

- I promise to work with colleagues across the aisle as my modus operandi from the beginning. I will not abandon my ideals, or values, but will honor other opinions on issues and when confronted with conflict and crisis work to compromise and negotiate.

- I care about the health and well being of Ohio's citizens, and pledge that I will help make The Affordable Care Act and its programs accessible and workable for all.

- I want to help Ohio's complex economy continue its recovery by supporting workers, farmers, small businesses, corporate investment, green technologies, and higher education. We must work together across complicated boundaries and possibilities to make our economic life stronger, more sustainable, and more responsible.

- I will help end the inconceivable assault on public schools and teachers during the past decade by drafting and passing a bi-partisan re-authorization of the Elementary and Secondary School Act (now known as NCLB) that eliminates high stakes testing and curbs the standardization of curriculum, teaching, and assessment and the privatizing influences of for-profit charters.

- I want us to invest more in higher education and students, so that all citizens have access to quality, meaningful, purposeful opportunities to learn, advance economically, and serve society.

- I will work with local, state, and federal entities to ensure the viability and maintenance of our infrastructure—a gift of service and sacrifice we give to the generations that follow—including good roads and bridges, transportation services, stable government services, financial standing.

- I want us to return to a thoughtful notion of how our work serves a public good—a common good—and not just individual goods. We have a responsibility to ourselves and future citizens to maintain and prosper a civil society that values hard work, sacrifice, education, families of all kinds, communities, cultures, and the arts with an eye toward the good of all, not just a select few.

I welcomed everyone to my home and to the meeting, and once everyone introduced themselves began discussing the platform. I would say that almost everyone in the room received the platform lukewarmly at best. One comment I made was that I wouldn't run for 13 months if it ceased to be fun, if it exacted such a toll so as to alienate me from others (especially friends); in fact, if it sucked the life out of me, if it killed me, I would quit. I meant it tongue in cheek. I wanted to make the point that this would be a different campaign. One guest said this,

> "You really shouldn't consider running for office if you want to have fun. Citizens don't want to hear about you having fun or care if it's fun for you. They want you to represent them. Fun has nothing to do with it."

"Wow," I thought to myself, "there's a person I definitely don't want working on this campaign." But out loud I said, "What I mean is that I want to surround myself with people who will enjoy the work and each other's company. I want this to be a positive experience for everyone. If I didn't want that, I would think there was something tremendously wrong with me. I like to work, and will work hard, but don't want it all to be such heavy lifting that it kills us. This process should give us life, and joy, and hope."

She was unmoved, as was most everyone else in the room. We moved on to less heady topics, the most important being, "Who's going to be your campaign manager?"

"Finding someone to do this will be the most difficult step," offered a leading county operative, himself having no interest in being my campaign manager.

"We know some people who could do it, but they are already booked on other campaigns," said another disinterested operative at the county level.

The person I immediately thought about was Ginger Simpson, my good friend sitting to my left at 11 o'clock. We discussed some people around the room, and Ginger's name came up. She had worked on several winning local school bond/levy campaigns.

She pushed the notion aside out loud, "I'm not really in any position at work to be able to do this as a volunteer, or to leave my job even if it were paid. The timing is just not good for me."

However, there was enough interest in her voice and obvious talent in her resume to make several people jump her after the meeting and encourage her to try it.

By the next morning Ginger was my campaign manager. What she was managing, I wasn't sure. But she came on board, as an unpaid volunteer, and that was great.

But I had that nagging feeling in my gut about the meeting, despite the good result of landing Ginger as my campaign manager, an awful feeling that I would get a million times over the next year: "That didn't go quite as I had planned. In fact, that did not go very well at all. Who in the hell is in charge here, after all? And what in the world are we doing?"

October 23, 2013

MIAMI UNIVERSITY'S COLLEGE DEMS

Ginger and I agreed that one of the key groups who would support me and give me a feel about whether or not I could even get into this race legitimately was the College Democrats. Official student groups on campus involved in politics included the College Republicans and the College Democrats. The formal Republican group far outnumbered the Democratic group on campus, but the Democrats, nonetheless, were robust, and had great interest in welcoming me to their weekly Wednesday night meeting for a short talk during their program. It's funny—regardless of how conservative Miami students and their parents seemed to be on a day-to-day basis—in the past, during presidential elections, the campus students typically went for the Democrat. Obama ran strong here in '08 and '12. Locals knew that passing any type of tax levy or bond for schools would be advantaged by the more progressive views of young people at the polls. And this panned out for the school district on several occasions. I was excited to meet them.

Because I'm a college professor and speak in front of groups of students all the time, I didn't feel as nervous or as much of a fish out of water as I would later in the campaign as the events got more important and the stakes higher (at least I thought the real stakes would be higher; I found out in actuality that they weren't!). I discussed several topics with Ginger before the meeting, agreed on some key talking points, and went in without notes.

I introduced myself:

"Good evening everyone, I'm Tom Poetter. I'm a faculty member in the Department of Educational Leadership. My field of study is Curriculum Studies. But tonight I'm a politician: I am running for congress against John Boehner in District 8 because he sacrificed any semblance of legitimate leadership when he let his own caucus bully him into shutting down the U.S. Government, ostensibly in a snit over the Affordable Care Act and President Obama's rightful position of not negotiating changes to a settled law so close to implementation."

The students liked that, and clapped, and spurred me on.

"It's time for a citizen-candidate to rise and represent the citizens of this great district. Boehner's never here, and he's lost touch with the thousands of people who do want health care, who do want representation, who don't want a government that is dysfunctional. They don't want someone who hates the government! We are the government. We are the people of District 8!"

Clapping. Then I settled down, spoke to them. "Our path to victory is very difficult, as you know. In the last contested election, in 2010—Boehner ran unopposed in 2012—the Democratic nominee running against Boehner got a meager 30% of the vote. So, you can do the math with me. If there are 200,000 votes in this district and Boehner got 135,000 and the challenger got only 65,000 in 2010, we have to turn around 40,000 votes to have a chance. That might seem impossible. Maybe it is, but we are going to try. And we need your help to do it! Will you join me in the fight?"

Yes! Applause.

"I need students on college campuses all over this district to take an interest in this campaign. I need you to tweet, and post on facebook, and start a grassroots campaign to unseat Boehner. We have to do this together. That's the only way to win a campaign, to do something meaningful, to change the equation about what counts for leadership in public office."

I took questions, and the questions from this robust group of about 40 students were tremendous. I didn't have many concrete answers, though I understood conceptually at least what I thought was important and where I stood with people and the basic issues. But I found out in these short moments just how much more I had to learn, issues I had to be conversant about.

"What do you think about Ohio's push for marriage rights?"

"Do you support protections for gay and lesbian couples in the workplace?"

"What about legalizing marijuana?"

"How would you suggest that we get a budget deal with all of the rancor?"

And the beat goes on. I blathered through some answers, but I knew that the speech had been fine—the q/a weak. I stayed for the entire meeting. Volunteers signed up to help us on the way out. I greeted and thanked as many students as I could face-to-face. We discussed briefly with the leadership group a date for a rollout event in the Uptown Park in November. We set a date on the fly for Tuesday November 19.

On the way to our cars, Ginger and I both felt energized. We knew we could do this now. The College Dems had given us the support we needed, and exposed many weaknesses, especially the fragile depth of my knowledge base on the issues.

We shook hands at the car and said goodnight.

"You can do this," Ginger said, a gleam in her eye. We shared the tense air of competition at the surface of our lives, taking us over.

"I think so, too." Tomorrow's events would reinforce this fact.

October 24, 2013
THE CHAIRMAN
CALLS

I didn't recognize the number ringing on my cell phone. I had already started to ignore most incoming calls if I didn't recognize the number. As a candidate, I didn't want to get caught by surprise. I didn't want to get stuck on the phone in a conversation I wasn't ready for. I couldn't waste any time talking with anyone I didn't have time for. That sounds snitty, and unconfident all at the same time. But I just couldn't do it.

The call was coming from the Columbus area code (614), so I took it for some reason, I'll never know exactly why. I had friends in Columbus; it could be any one of them whose number I had never added to my phone.

"Tom, Hi, it's Chris Redfern, Chair of the Ohio Democratic Party. How are you?"

"I'm well, sir. Yes, well, to tell the truth, I'm surprised to hear from you. I didn't know anyone in Columbus had even heard of me. What can I do for you?"

"I've known about you from the beginning, Tom. I'm calling to tell you that *Newsweek* wants to interview the man running against the Speaker of the House. I told them that person was you, and you'll be getting a call shortly from them."

"Well, sir, I'm honored that you feel that I'm the person for the job, but I haven't taken any steps to formally announce anything. I barely have a team together."

"Believe me, Tom, you're running. Let me know how the interview goes."

"Thank you, Sir, I will. I'm assuming I can count on your support no matter how the *Newsweek* interview turns out?"

"You'll do great, Tom. Stay in touch." Click.

I called Ginger.

She raced over and we started to prepare for the interview.

My stomach churned, and so did my mind.

"This is real."

"How will I keep from screwing this up?"

"What if I gaffe, or can't answer the questions?"

The call from the reporter came at 1:30 pm. After a few minutes I felt at ease. Most of the questions were lob balls, easy to hit. "What made you get in the race? What kind of political experience do you have? What can we expect from your campaign? Do you have any skeletons in your closet that you would like to get out at the beginning?"

"I'm the cleanest candidate to run for this seat in 80 years. I have nothing to hide, and nothing in my background that is questionable. That's not the case for my opponent, but it is for me."

People who read the article couldn't stop talking about the "cleanest candidate in 80 years" line. I thought it held up well, though some old standbys in Oxford thought it marginalized everyone else on our side who had run for the office over the years. I just responded, "It doesn't matter who it is, or what side they're on. I'm cleaner."

That was the truth. An indisputable fact. It didn't translate into any votes won in the long run, but it was true.

I got an instant round of contacts coming in the next day when the piece appeared online. Emails and calls came flooding in. People didn't know where to send money, how could they do that? Where was my website? What was my platform? What issues did I care about? How did I plan to beat Boehner? What kinds of other relevant experience did I have? Why did I think I had any chance against him?

It became a fact of the matter that these questions continued throughout the campaign. People just wanted to know more about me. Why should we vote for you? What do you stand for? Where did you come from? What are your chances? Etc.

Instantly we realized that we had absolutely no digital infrastructure in a digital age. We had spent weeks deciding whether or not to run. Now we needed to take very, very swift next steps to build a digital imprint for the campaign. The very first thing we had to be able to do was take in campaign contributions. I needed a treasurer just to file the papers to run with the Federal Election Commission (FEC) and we needed to be connected to a donation site like ActBlue.org. We needed a web page built immediately and we needed some initial content to go up there besides the typical call for help to support the campaign.

I turned to several friends to help us do this, volunteers who wouldn't get paid that I staked everything on in terms of trust and expertise. They came through the best they could by creating an adequate infrastructure to get started. I stressed that we had to get it right from the beginning, and that I couldn't do it myself.

We built a website that could do what we needed it to do overnight. We created a link so that donors could go to ActBlue and make a donation with their credit card. We got a bank account opened so that donors could write a check and mail it to our treasurer.

I wrote to all my friends on email and asked them to make a donation.

We raised about $5,000 in the first week. Much leaner times would come.

MIND NUMBING
OBSTACLES

So much happened so fast. I took Ginger and my good friend Marvin—
who had volunteered to be my initial treasurer and who would see me though
some dark days of the campaign as a close friend—to see the County Party
Chair, Nicole Mantle, for coffee. The chair was known as an operative with
experience, having served on several winning federal campaigns in other
states, settling in this county after quitting Washington and building a new
local political career. We hadn't met her yet face-to-face; we had only spoken
on the phone and email. Big moment.

When we met, we shook hands, sat down, and she asked me point blank,
"So why are you running for congress?" My hot chocolate nearly burned my
hands through the paper cup, no time to cool, as I fumbled around.

I stumbled through a couple of sentences and she mercifully stopped
me. She said, "First of all, you aren't going to ever say the words 'progressive
impulse' or 'blue wave' again. You can't get elected saying those phrases."

"And being a college professor doesn't help you, it hurts you. Downplay
that. Education may be your strong suit, but being a college professor puts
you out of touch with the average voter."

"You have to have a strong, compelling, automatic elevator speech con-
taining the points you care about, why you are doing this, who you are, how
you plan to win."

"And you can't run a campaign just in Oxford. It's such a small percent of the vote in the district. You have to win votes in Hamilton and Middletown and Troy and Greenville and Springfield, not Oxford. You are going to win Oxford, so that can't be your focal point."

"It's great you have a campaign manager, but you need to focus on raising money. You need a finance director right away. And you don't need to spend a lot of money on a website. Just get something up and running that people can find so that they can donate to your campaign. Content can come later. About money, **you are to spend nothing on anything** until you have some and then you aren't to spend it on anything but Boehner."

"There are other Democrats who might run even if you are in the race. You need to be aware of them and get them to work for you and not run against you if you can. It doesn't mean you won't have a primary, because almost anyone can run in these primaries in Ohio. You don't even have to live in the district to run. You just need 50 good signatures, file on time, and to pay the fee in order to be certified to the ballot."

"You need to make connections with the best people in our county and get them to work for you, and you have to connect with the other five county chairs in the district. They will be key in helping you create an infrastructure for your campaign."

We took notes furiously. Marv appeared to have gotten caught in the headlights, his eyes glazing over. Too much too soon. It would only get worse. I felt sharp, but overwhelmed. I wanted Nicole to like me, to think I could do this.

I asked, "What do you think of me so far? Do you think I can do this?"

"Anyone can run for congress. What you have to show is that you are in this to win, that you have ideas, and that you can put in the work. You have to make phone calls to raise money. Only you can do that. Donors won't just give to you because you are running against Boehner. You will have to convince them on the phone. You have to knock on doors in a huge geographic district, thousands of doors. You have to do that. You will have to make speeches and go to events and build a campaign staff, which might be tested in just a few months in the May primary. You have to do all of that and more."

"You have to raise at least $1 million to win, really to have any chance whatsoever. You can't possibly raise that much, though. I don't think you can raise $100,000, but let's shoot for that. You might think it is early to run with a year to go, but it's actually very late. In order to raise enough money to compete, you should have gotten in this race at least six months ago."

"You are married to a Republican, for 27 years. That helps. You are an ordained minister. That helps. For now, those are the only two things I would talk about. They help you. Everything else, including being a Democrat, I'm sorry to say, hurts you. You are running against the most powerful Republican in the nation, in one of the nation's reddest districts."

My impressions of the chair formed in those several minutes and they never changed over the course of the next year as we built a relationship and then let politics squash it like a bug. She was experienced, smart, and helpful. She was quick to form an opinion and to share it. She could be generous with her time and insights, but she wouldn't suffer fools for very long if even for an instant.

She took out a piece of paper and wrote down a phone number. She slipped it to me across the table. "Here is Bill Higby's phone number. He is planning to run, too, unless you contact him to work something out. Do it right away. If you have any questions, call me. I'll be happy to help out any way I can."

She said all of this with a smile. And she meant it, though I couldn't have imagined in that moment all of the strings attached, to every word and every idea …

Overwhelmed, my team drove home in silence.

October 29, 2013

LUNCH
WITH BILL

I wasted no time getting ahold of Bill Higby, a Democrat in Butler County—who hated the Tea Party vehemently, who had become extremely agitated by the government shutdown, who had managed a congressional campaign in another state already, and who had decided to run against Boehner if no one else got in the race. He had heard about me from Nicole, appreciated the quick phone call from me, and agreed to meet with me for lunch. My treat.

We met in Millville, about halfway between his home and mine, and got right down to it. He tried to impress me with his knowledge and experience. It worked; I liked Bill, and thought he had a lot to offer. I wanted to put him to work as political director immediately. He wanted to manage the campaign, but I already had Ginger. He agreed to accept a lesser role, though I could tell even this early that he was the kind of person who would push as many buttons as possible moving forward to challenge Boehner and would probably tire of taking orders from the top and pine to be in charge. I pitched "team effort," and he agreed to it in principle, but I worried from the word "go" that it wouldn't be enough. It wasn't.

"I can't stand Boehner, and the Tea Party, and the destruction they have brought to national and local politics. Boehner hasn't done anything for Butler County, his home base. He needs to go, he's tired and has no ideas.

He's a power monger and the leader of a rogue congress. This has to stop. I want to help you do it." At that moment I knew that he had been cleared from the field as a competitor.

Bill could devote time to the campaign and wanted to jump right in. He claimed to have technology skills, that he could build a new website, that he would get the word out on Facebook and Twitter, and perhaps bring the campaign into the 21st century. He had run a congressional campaign in another state in 2012, helping the man known as "the junkyard dog," who raised very little money and barely campaigned—to win a tightly contested primary and to run more "legitimately" in the Fall election. Bill told the story noted below, I think in hopes of convincing me that he was excited about "moving up" to help me out. I don't think he thought he could get any lower, though the experience for him had been foundational as he had worked on many past campaigns but never ran one before this one. He was no stranger to regional Democratic politics. He told his best story about managing that campaign:

"I never knew where my candidate would be. He could be on the road anywhere in the country looking for materials for his junkyard. He had an undependable cell phone with bad service and he wouldn't answer it if he didn't want to. What a throwback, a nice guy who wanted to serve but had no idea what to do or how to do it. I worked my ass off to get a meeting for him with Vice President Biden on the tarmack when the VP was landing for a talk just a few weeks before the 2012 general election. What a great break for us to get a few minutes with Mr. Biden and the photo op and support of the Vice President of the United States of America!"

"And the plane lands, and my guy is no where in sight. I was frantically calling him, when Biden's advance people come off the plane to meet me, and start talking about where Biden will take the meeting with us, and I had to admit as they were talking and directing me that I didn't have him in hand. They got pissed, and said they couldn't go back on that plane and tell the Vice President that my candidate had stood him up. I apologized and started calling him again, and he finally answers from the cab of his truck. He's in Nebraska trying to buy a closed junkyard! Now I'm screaming at him, 'The Vice President is getting off a plane to see you in two minutes.' He hung up. What could he say?"

"He just flat out didn't care, didn't get it, and did his own thing, God love him. It didn't matter if it was the Vice President of the United States—he had junk to tend to."

I loved that story. I actually joked that Bill wouldn't have to worry about me missing a meeting with the vice president if we ever got a chance like that.

But from the beginning I was wary. I like opinionated, strong people who like to collaborate. I think Bill fit that bill. But I also thought he may be too radical, maybe too volatile for me. I wondered how he would behave under pressure, how he would take direction from a political novice like me. Could he be loyal, devoted?

But I guessed if he stuck it out with the junk yard dog candidate who left him embarrassed on a tarmack with the Vice President's men swearing him down, then I probably couldn't do anything worse to him. Of course, I was wrong.

November 8, 2013

TRIVIA NIGHT

Time passes so slowly, and so quickly on a campaign.

On the one hand, I plowed along with life as it just streamed by with day turning to night in a seeming heartbeat, trying to do my job at Miami, to raise two teenage boys, to be a decent husband, to look after the home and our finances, and to run a congressional campaign! We had meetings each week at our home on Wednesday evenings, and they had been going fairly well. We had been making plans for a rally to officially kick off the campaign on November 19th in Oxford's uptown park. We got a permit for that, and recruited a local musician to provide warm up music. We bought an early ad for the event in the local paper and hoped with our connections that we could get 200 or 300 people there for the event. Pipe dreams.

And everything just slowed down to a crawl, all at the same time that the world flew by in a whirlwind. Every day felt like a trial, a million new things to learn, people to rein in, events to plan, calls to make, emails to write, positions to take, issues to learn about and stand for, etc., etc. Each one of those things had a lead up time with planning and then the meeting and then a debriefing. Every thing we did took so much time and effort, dragging on and on, and flying by. One of the weighty things that has an impact on time is knowing that you are so far behind with only baby steps to take to make up the difference in money raised (impossible), expertise (growing, but still not congressional seat ready), and infrastructure (we had a campaign manager, political director, and treasurer—but all volunteers not working full time, including the candidate!). Even this early I felt snowed under by the workload of the campaign and everything else on top of it. How could I keep up the pace? How could I get everything done, do it well, and on time? How would I ever be prepared enough for the next meeting, the next talk, the next rally, the next phone call?

And so the Butler County Progressives invited me to my first "public event," its first ever Trivia Night. The group organizes events for members and encourages participation in politics, inviting speakers in at opportune times. The leadership thought it would be a good time to introduce me to 50 or so Butler County Democrats. I could make my elevator speech along with several other candidates and have a casual night of fun with politics.

As a social person, with many years of public and private experiences of being either the life of the party or at least very, very comfortable in almost any social setting, this first public event was extremely awkward, unsatisfying, and probably would have caused almost anybody else to quit on the spot.

The first, worst thing to happen is that I walked up to a table of four young people in their 20s, none of whom I knew, handed out a palm card to each one, intending to make my rounds of each of the tables set up for the event, and said, "Hi, I'm Tom Poetter. I'm running for congress against John Boehner."

They just looked up at me blankly in a completely uniform, negative cloud of disgust. They didn't say a word for the most awkward few seconds in history.

Nonplussed, I said, "No, really, I'm running for congress. I hope you'll join our campaign to unseat the speaker. I would really appreciate your help."

They just laughed, and turned back to each other and giggled and went about talking amongst themselves. They didn't say a word to me, barely even looking up. Then I said, now clearly agitated, "No, <u>really</u>, I want to know what you care about and what I can do to help this district. I would love for you to volunteer to help me out."

After all, these were supposed to be my people. Butler County Progressives.

One of the males took the only verbal swing necessary to shut me up, "Look, man, good luck. But we came for the trivia, not for politics."

Welcome to the voting public.

I boiled inside. I never got over the fact that the first people I met on the campaign trail thought I was a joke, and cared nothing about politics. They joined the cast of many thousands of people I met in person and on the phone who didn't give a damn about the political process, had their minds made up already, or just wanted to be left alone with their own thoughts on matters. Indifferent.

Whatever. This was very difficult to absorb and interpret, to understand.

I recovered as quickly as I could. I went to the next table. I started over again. I went to every table. I said what I was doing, and hardly anyone cared.

The trivia was miserable. I don't mind games, but it dragged on and on. Finally, the organizer came over and said to me, "During the scoring session, you can stand up and give your speech. You ready?"

Sure.

I spoke for about 90 seconds. All of it lame and forced and not magical. I wasn't funny. No one cared about my race. It was trivia night!

I thought, "Could I even possibly learn to do this?" I thought I had talent, appeal. I was kind and passionate and thoughtful. Fact is, none of it mattered at Trivia Night. By the way, my trivia team got killed and almost came in last. A familiar mantra.

Hometown
Fireworks

During the early weeks of the campaign, I attempted to carefully put the pieces together for a campaign committee that I thought would serve throughout the campaign as a beacon, a guide. We met at my home around the kitchen table for the first six weeks.

Quaint. And awful.

My wife Chris hated having everyone crawling all over her space after work and for long hours on Wednesday nights. I didn't blame her, especially after this meeting. I knew afterward that we had to get out of the house and set up our work in an office space. The notion of running a campaign out of the house made (in)famous by Jason Zone Fisher's (2008) documentary *Swing State*—about Ted Strickland and Lee Fisher's ascension to the Ohio Governor's mansion in 2006, in part through Lee's living room!—had no chance of succeeding in my world. The Poetter campaign completely wore out its welcome in the house by the end of the night.

People started arriving right around the time Chris got home from work. Though not officially part of the meeting, Chris saw it all go down.

I had invited people to this meeting who would comprise what I thought would be my central campaign committee, made up of the people I had determined to have close at hand helping throughout the campaign. Max Smith and Cindy Winter, Butler County political veterans from numerous campaigns. Initially, I was really glad to have both of these experienced party members there. Max had actually attended earlier meetings; this was Cindy's first. I thought we needed their expertise and track record to run. Larry Barr and Mary Stinson were Oxford progressives who had been heavily involved in democratic politics. Burt was democratic operative who had helped to get me into this mess with the first email. Bill was my new political director. Ginger, my campaign manager. My new treasurer couldn't make it, and Marv was trying to decide if he could do the job of finance director, so he didn't appear. He was still suffering from shell shock from our first meeting with Nicole, which made him very wary of taking a formal role in the campaign. All eight of us squeezed in around the table: Bill, Ginger, Cindy, Max, Larry, Mary, Burt, and Tom.

Only one of us would be left standing by mid-February 2014, just a few months off. Take a guess who …

The agenda seemed very clear to me. I spoke from my chair. "Thank you all for coming tonight. Please take pizza and drinks as you please. Let's spend the first part of the meeting putting the finishing touches on our campaign kick off event."

Cindy cut me off right there. She put her hand up to stop me from talking. I stopped. I think I immediately fell into shock and blind rage all at the same time. I'm not sure I had ever had anyone put a hand up in a meeting to stop me from talking, at least an occasion that wasn't clearly a joke or an all out invitation for a fist fight. Cindy and I had met only briefly on the phone; this was our first face-to-face meeting.

"First of all, Tom, Ginger needs to be running this meeting if she is going to be the campaign manager. You don't run the meetings. You are the candidate."

Awkward. Whose house was this? Who in the hell are you?

She turned to Ginger, "You need to make the agenda, you tell Tom what to do, and you get this organization up and running. You provide the leadership."

I could feel Bill trembling next to me. He immediately jumped in.

"This is your first meeting, Cindy. We know what we are doing. I have already run a congressional campaign myself. We are doing fine without your critique," he was visually and verbally upset, his voice shaking.

I was pissed off. I didn't like her tone and her approach, either.

Ginger said, "I can run the meeting, Cindy. But we have a long relationship, Tom and I. I like him and trust him and am willing to follow his lead until we get some things figured out, including who does what. I'm very comfortable with him starting a meeting."

Un-phased by these relatively polite and immediate rebukes, Cindy launched into a 10-minute harangue about how campaign committees are run, who does what jobs, how we were hopelessly behind and didn't know what we were doing. None of this was on my agenda.

Across the table I could tell that Larry and Mary and Burt loved Cindy and the conflict. Their eyes danced. Ginger and Bill hated her immediately. The rest of the meeting we argued and jockeyed and defended. All of us setting up camp and trying to establish ourselves. This was supposed to be my committee, the best people in the county who were supposed to help me and become my friends. They were supposed to help me run against Boehner. I needed friends, and aides, and support. I didn't want sycophants. But I didn't want enemies, either. But I would not sacrifice friendship and goodwill for expertise. Perhaps that makes me an immediate loser. So be it.

The climax of pain came when Larry pressed me to voice my platform. I said, "You've heard me do that before at other meetings, I have written it all out, it's sitting right in front of you. I'm not spending any time rehearsing for you or proving myself." I was really, totally pissed off now. Vehement. But he pressed anyway. I threw up my hands and started to list off a string of things I cared about, almost facetiously. Then more debate, more disagreement, more conflict. We got nowhere, got nothing done. This group would never meet again, but on the way out, both Burt and Larry shook my hand vigorously and said, "What a great meeting. Best ever." Clearly, they loved the Cindy Winter show, a one-night performance that would provide pain, and clarity, for months to come.

CAMPAIGN
KICKOFF

Plans for our opening rally in the uptown park in Oxford took shape even though our final planning meeting went south the week before. I had envisioned that more than 100 College Democrats would march with signs of support from campus into uptown Oxford for the event at the park on the town square. At the dragging end of the semester, despite the early solid turnout at the October meeting, only about 10 students straggled to the event. So incredibly disappointing.

We hurried to get a logo done by an artist and an 8' banner suitable for hanging at events and carrying in parades. We also had had palm cards made that would last throughout the campaign. They worked fine, though later when we got a better logo we didn't invest in new palm cards. The banner arrived in time and city workers hung the banner on the bandstand in the uptown park where the event would take place. The banner flew for all to see all day in the bright, cold November sunshine, visible to all.

A good friend texted me that he had seen the sign while driving uptown, but unfortunately that my name had been misspelled.

I rushed uptown to view the sign and get it taken down, if need be. Of course, the sign was perfect. My friend just wanted me to keep my britches the right size. I laughed and laughed. That helped as the nerves really began to build.

A few weeks earlier I had booked Jack Metz, a local musician, to play warm up music for the crowd ahead of the event. I offered him $150 for the performance, which he accepted. A member of my planning team had agreed to pay him out of his own pocket, then reneged at the last minute. But Jack got paid, and so did the sound and light team that came to help set up and run the show.

I had been writing and rehearsing my speech for about a week. I thought it was 12 minutes long. I decided that I had to read it, that I just didn't have enough confidence to speak from the heart and make it through the material extemporaneously, with just notes at hand. That meant I had to find a lectern, which is a really hard item to find. I got one at the church, loaded it in the car, and delivered it to the event myself. Ginger and others bought cookies and drinks, and set up a table. The Butler County Progressives, who had sponsored trivia night, showed up to seed the crowd and hold up its sign.

We had advertised the event on social media and with a quarter page ad in the weekly paper, *The Oxford Press*.

By the time the 6 pm start time had rolled around, it was getting dark, and really cold. The temperature got down below freezing by the time we started, and we knew the weather kept people away. But we couldn't help that.

One of the great things that happened was meeting eight members of the Democratic Party from Miami County. My new friends had come all the way from Troy together in a van (about a 90 minute drive) to see the event and support my kickoff. What a treat hosting them after their long trip.

About 80 people had assembled when Burt introduced me. He did a nice job and I was on. I was disappointed in the crowd. But what more could we do? Why couldn't I attract even 100 people in my hometown to an event?

I made several mistakes during the speech. I mentioned thanks to many people, but forgot to mention Nicole, the Butler County Democratic Chair, the most powerful Democrat in the region, and a strong advisor and friend so far, who had shown up for the event. I just forgot. And, of course, I read my speech. It went fine, but Chris afterward said, "You are better when you just speak from the heart." Maybe, but I just couldn't.

At a significant point near the end of the speech, I got stuck on a word and it all tumbled out wrong. I botched the closing, and it was noticeable. The videotape of the event taken by a supporter was ruined. I didn't know how to edit the film and we just let it go. Another mistake among many made so early and so prominently.

After the event I joined several people in an uptown bar, and we talked and laughed and people said nice things about how the event went and how well things were going. To be honest, I was just so glad it was over. But I knew there were so many more of these events to come. In fact, I was due at the Clark County Democratic Party Meeting the next night at 8 pm.

Certainly, recalling a cold, uneven night like this, one that foretold how things could go so wrong in a heartbeat, and how mistakes would be magnified, things would soon snowball out of control. I found out early that I controlled so much, and so little all at the same time as I bounced around as a candidate for the first time in my life.

It became clear to me that while I thought that John Boehner was my opponent, the fact was that I was the opponent, as well as my organization, my friends, and my party. Convincing them, winning them, became a full time job. I hardly had time to focus, and to learn.

November 20, 2013

CLARK
COUNTY DEMS

A few weeks earlier, Burt had volunteered to drive me to some early events, and when I mentioned the Clark County Party meeting he volunteered to take me up. This is all part of the mystique of candidate use of time that never sat well with me the entire campaign. Staffers and volunteers who acted like they knew what they were doing and what the candidate should do always argued that I should never drive anywhere on my own once I was the candidate. One argument was the "no trouble" clause; while the candidate may get a sense of freedom from driving him or herself, it places the candidate at risk. The problems associated with speeding tickets, parking tickets, and accidents are too hard to overcome especially when they happen in the heat of the campaign. Driving means trouble; not driving means "no trouble." Another argument is that driving is a waste of time, meaning if you are driving, then you aren't dialing the phone for dollars …

My main problem with having someone drive me throughout the campaign is that most people are terrible drivers and I don't feel safe with them. Or they annoy me or scare me, driving too fast or slow or possessing poor judgment. Another problem was that I didn't care to give anyone the satisfaction of simply "acting" like a real candidate by doing something or not doing something for no good reason. There's this powerful, romantic notion of the candidate sitting in the back seat dialing the phone, making the most efficient use of time, sucking every bit of bone marrow possible out of a campaign timeframe. Campaign operatives love being seen with the candidate getting out of the back seat after the driver opens the door. Vanity. Stupid. Over the course of the campaign, especially after this night, I drove almost everywhere we went on the campaign: to meetings, to speeches, to county fairs, to party picnics, to fundraisers, to knock on doors. If we had to drive, and we almost always had to do so, I drove.

But on this night, Burt drove and he drove poorly. And it's a long way to Springfield from Oxford. It took us more than two hours, and we were late, leaving as soon as possible after teaching my 4 pm class. We got a little lost, and when Burt tried to do a quick U-turn to get us back on track we nearly got broadsided by a truck speeding in the other direction. I almost kicked Burt out of the car that moment. I was actually shaken up a little bit by how close a call it was. But I had a speech to give.

When we got to the Hall, the meeting had already started. John Byron, the county chair, recognized me and said hi, interrupting the meeting. I felt a little more at home saying hi back and to the group and settled in just listening for a few moments. I had spoken to many people in this group a few weeks earlier at a fundraiser for the Democratic candidate for governor. The chair gave me a few minutes at that event and I made the most of it, making an impassioned plea for support ahead of the keynote speech. So tonight I had a little bit of confidence from the opening event the night before, and I knew the crowd a little bit, and I had my notes. What could go wrong?

Everything. I talked for about 10 minutes, trying to make some strides with the crowd, to get them excited about my points and planks and platform. Nothing. Very little interest. No questions. I will never, ever be able to understand how it's possible to give the same basic talk one night and basically hit it out of the park and on the next night fall flat on your face. That must be what comedians feel like when they go on stage. After these first few events, they barely got easier. I never knew what the crowd would do, or what they wanted. Yes, I'm good on my feet, but playing this game was like taking shots in the dark, blindfolded.

I stayed after and shook hands and said hello to everyone I could and passed out palm cards. I asked those gathered if they could organize a fundraiser for us in Springfield, like the one the governor candidate had a few weeks before. "Yes!" they said, but they would have to get back to me. I should have known better.

When we got in the car, I asked Burt what he thought about my talk. He said, "Well, it went fine, but you'll need to polish up your presentation." I agreed, and though I was exhausted and needed to relax, Burt wouldn't have any of it. He said, "I just want you to know that this is my last night on the campaign. I agreed to do this event tonight, and didn't want to let you down. But I can't drive you anywhere or support you in any other way either from here on out." I said, "Fine." Truly, I didn't really care.

Though he couldn't get enough of Cindy Winter, whom he idolized and who wreaked havoc in her first and last meeting with the team, I guess that wasn't a big enough draw to keep him active on the campaign. But he wouldn't leave it at that, starting and finishing a long, winding story of coming of age in college while working on an early campaign for John Gilligan, former U.S. Representative and Governor of Ohio.

"I remember seeing him the first time give a speech, and it was electric. What a thrill being around greatness, that talent." Obviously, I was no John Gilligan in Burt's eyes. And he had no interest in helping me get there. He started this whole thing with the email blast, and now a month later, it's over. Just like many others to come. The flighty, unstable, volatile nature of volunteers' commitment never ceased to amaze me over the course of the entire campaign.

November 21, 2013

SGT. PEPPER'S LONELY HEARTS CLUB BAND

David Pepper ran for attorney general in Ohio against Mike DeWine in 2014. He got killed in the election. But he was a great candidate. And ultimately, after the bloodbath for almost all Democrats in Ohio in 2014 (except for the four reverse "gerrymandered" U.S. Representatives from Ohio, residing and serving in places that Republicans can't win so the blue territory is simply ceded to Democrats), he was elected the new Ohio Democratic Party Chair.

The first time I met David was at a house fundraiser for him in Oxford tonight. The locals invited me to give a warm up talk. It would be the last fundraiser I would agree to speak at if I weren't the cause for the party. I just couldn't waste any more time and energy talking to people at parties in Oxford if those in attendance weren't there to support or help me. I knew them all already! And I would ask all of them for money at some point. As you can imagine, this would become a sore spot for local operatives who wanted me to spend all my time in Oxford where I was destined, by default, to do well at the polls no matter! And even if I could win more votes at home, there were so few to win as to make the investment of time and energy indefensible. After all, only 3% of the entire voting population in the district resided in Oxford.

After the hosts said a few nice words about my race and about me personally, I took the floor, and tried to get the body of Democrats in that room stirred up, excited. I spoke from the heart, without notes. I talked for about five minutes about Boehner's lack of leadership, his lack of presence in the district, his utter folly at bowing to right wing nuts and shutting down the government, the most despicable, heinous act possible for a public servant. I mentioned that the ACA would work, was working, would save us money, and would change the notion of health and well being in society. Not only the rich would have access to healthcare, and we wouldn't have to pay the astronomical final bills of the poor whose wallets couldn't pay for the biopsy that would have saved their lives. And their lives mattered. And a few more sentences, and a whimsical, hopeful line or two about being the underdog. And that was that.

I thought that was what I was supposed to do. Give a few remarks. Tell a bit about who I was and why I was running. I knew everyone in the room. Friends in the room applauded for me and smiled, which was nice, and then it was David's turn.

I stood to the side, close enough to practically touch him, and he started. The talk was masterful, and long. He told about his upbringing, who he was as a person, what he thought of incumbent Attorney General Mike Dewine's undisciplined use of taxpayer money to chase political cases, and to not spend the time necessary to defend every person's rights and causes in our state. And on and on the talk went, with excruciating detail. I have to admit, I loved the talk, but I could feel my knees buckling as the room got hot and the talk went on and on. Later someone told me the talk lasted 45 minutes. Amazing. It didn't seem like forever, but I was sweating at the end, and so was David.

I marveled at the length of the talk, the detail, the depth, and the smoothness of his delivery. No notes, all memorized, masterful. Like the young but seasoned politician he is, David took every opportunity he had, including the ones where people wrote him checks in support of his campaign, to impress the audience, to reveal his intellect, to tell his story, and to win the room. He would go on to raise several million dollars, all across Ohio in rooms like this one and bigger ones, and on the phone. A real pro, and a nice guy. I had so much to learn.

Everyone applauded, and wrote him a check if they hadn't already, and he cleaned up. He left soon after his talk, didn't stay around long talking with others, but I lingered and talked and yucked it up with the faithful.

No one gave me a dime.

The people in that room could have written us both checks of the same amount and no one would have felt it in their mortgage payment, or their next trip to the store. Nothing. Not a cent.

I knew this wasn't my fundraiser. But I told the crowd during my remarks that for us to have a chance we had to raise several hundred thousand dollars. It was the first time that I heard guffawing in my presence. But wait a minute. How was this possible? Here I was building a citizen's campaign. I was no slouch, but unseasoned and green as a politician. Didn't the people in that room just hand Pepper $100 or $250 without blinking an eye for a campaign that would raise several million dollars? And I was trying to mount a decent campaign with nothing.

Why wouldn't everyone in that room pony up? They were Democrats, couldn't stand Boehner, and I was taking on the task. There are so many answers to this question of why not ... For starters, I hadn't done anything to earn their support. Throwing my hat in the ring meant basically nothing to them. Like any beginning candidate, obviously I could fall out of the race at any time. And I took for granted that people knew me and would support me just because of who I am and what I had done in my work and in the community. But absolutely no one cared anything about any of that. What qualities as a person did I have that made me a better choice than Boehner, besides simply being a Democrat? Why should they invest their hard earned cash in me? Many of them wouldn't. None of them did tonight.

November 26, 2013

CALL TIME

The Ohio Democratic Party sent us an initial phone list of donors. The list was long, unorganized. It was a general list of Ohio donors, some who had given to the party, some to federal and state senate and representative races, some to statewide office races, some to Obama, etc. To date, we really didn't know anything about how to plan for, research, and start a substantive phone-based money raising campaign for a political run like the one we had taken on. We would have to learn this process, through many hard lessons, over time. And new talent would have to join the team to get us there.

So without much practice, but with the pressing need to raise money, I started calling people on this list as well as friends and family members. The biggest expense on the horizon was renting office space for the campaign, but, of course, that was just the tip of the iceberg in terms of future expenditures. I really had no idea what I was in for …

As a novice, I listened to what my staff and others in the county told me about raising money over the phone:

- 9 out of 10 calls, or maybe even 99 out of 100 calls on any given day, would fail.
- I would have to call back many of the people who had already said "no" to me.
- You start with a short script that becomes natural with practice.

- Getting the person interested in the race on the phone is a big step, but equally important is "closing," asking for a donation and getting the money over the phone (credit card), or getting a commitment to a particular amount.

- Middle class people on these lists give money to political campaigns, so don't be embarrassed to ask them for a sizeable donation to take on the work ahead.

- Time is money; the more you dial, the more you make.

I had all kinds of trouble with "call time"—what campaign staffers call the time spent dialing donors, or phone fundraising. I hated that I had to spend time on the phone essentially selling myself to people I had never met. Basically, cold calling. I wondered how my psyche would handle the criticism, the uncertainty, and the failure. My wonder turned quickly to answers: I didn't handle it very well at all. Call time haunted me, loomed over me like a fixed point of death on the horizon every single day, every single minute. When I first got into it, I had no idea how devastating call time would be, and ultimately (which I hate to admit) how exhilarating.

I called people who laughed at me (sometimes this was a nervous reflex, sometimes the person was just mean). I called people who hung up on me. I called people who told me that I was crazy for running against Boehner and was wasting their time. And much worse. Overall, I faced several challenges with call time that I'm still dealing with as a human being who survived this political campaign, somewhat in tact.

The first challenge was just getting experience, learning how to do it. I can't tell you how many times I fumbled, stumbled over my opening line, "Hello, Louise. My name is Tom Poetter, I'm running for congress against John Boehner in Ohio's 8th District. How are you today?" Even amidst the utter failure of the enterprise, small victories loomed, and it led to questioning whether I was any good at it or not. Staffers said it didn't matter whether I was good at it or not. All that mattered was volume, the number of calls I made. If I made the calls, we would make money. Of course, I would get better at it with time and experience. Any donkey would. This wasn't about talent or ideas or politics. This was about putting in the time.

The second challenge was forcing myself to show up and do call time. When you face a continual dose of failure in an enterprise, with very little success, at least at first, it's hard to keep going back. One of the great tests in politics is dealing with failure. I have always dealt with failure poorly in my life, letting it upset me, then working hard to reverse the feeling with greater effort. Not quitting is good in politics, but it leads to more and more bad experiences, more and more failures. The average person, like me, is not built for this.

I met all kinds of politicians, some who had little coaching or drive and had no idea what I even meant by "call time" and some who called people on the phone asking for money 6–10 hours a day, in a disciplined, focused way, and raised a lot of cash. I personally could only stomach three hours of call time a day. For me, dialing myself, that amounted to approximately 100 calls a day. This is not herculean, and it's not nothing. But it's what I could do without driving my car into a tree. Literally, call time is the most devastating activity in politics.

When you do the math, counting the stray calls I made at this early moment, the beginning of the campaign, and then estimating the number based on the time I spent per week on the phone from March through October 2014, I made over 20,000 phone calls to potential donors. That's well over 600 hours of call time, estimated, in just over a year-long campaign. 15 complete work weeks. An entire semester of work.

The third, and biggest challenge, was asking friends and family members for money. I didn't realize the magnitude of this until much later, but I knew in my craw at the beginning that asking for money would have a devastating impact on my personal life. Everyone said the base of your campaign is the money friends and family put in. Most said a middle class candidate like me should raise 40–50K just from friends. To do this, I had to call everyone I knew. This meant that many of them would say no. They didn't have the money (they did), they didn't believe in my race, they weren't Democrats, or they just didn't give to politicians. But when I asked them to help me, I put our friendship on the line. If I asked, and the person didn't give, our relationship ended. I felt as though running for congress is rare, and when a friend asks for money to do it, as little as $25 isn't too much to ask. It's a confirmation of the task, of your relationship, of the effort. It's the bare minimum you can do when asked, regardless. It mattered to me that people confirmed our connection. If they didn't, I severed it. Truth.

November 29, 2013

SANCTUARY

Like with football, Sam's activities in high school, in this case varsity ice hockey, provided a sanctuary for me during the winter months of the campaign. In fact, when a local would ask me why I wasn't at so and so's Christening or at so and so's baby shower or at so and so's square dance or at so and so's birthday party or at so and so's funeral (for real), or whatever, I simply said, "I have a full-time job, a family with one boy in college and one boy still in high school, and a wife who is not a widow, yet. I won't be campaigning on the following dates: List of dates ..." Before everything would change so drastically with the campaign in March of 2014, I was able to spend some days with family, most often days Sam played hockey. This allowed for some decompression and fun and life. I don't know what I would have done if Sam didn't play high school sports! Truth is, I may have lost my family and myself completely.

Unfortunately, I violated my "days off" rule this weekend, right after Thanksgiving, the traditional weekend for the high school's annual invitational hockey tournament held here in town. I had it planned that we would do what we always do: Go to see Chris' folks in St. Marys, celebrate Thanksgiving, come home on Friday, and take the boys to the hockey games on Friday, Saturday, and Sunday. Between the games, we would go to the bi-annual sports card and memorabilia show held in Cincinnati and eat ribs at Montgomery Inn. A blast. We did all of that and more, and really enjoyed ourselves. But I still had a run-in on the phone, completely unable to distance myself safely from the campaign for any significant length of time. And this interaction would make me question my entire approach, and really make me miserable. I carried the phone event with me for months. I wondered, like the caller, "Was I all in?"

The phone event: We had been talking long distance with a former Democratic campaign for a house seat in a northern Ohio district, one that had been very successful in raising money in a year, making and spending over $1 million in a losing race. I know that if you are reading this you may be comparing that seemingly small number to the exorbitant amount raised by presidential candidates in the '16 races. Yes, the presidential campaigns can make $1 million seem small. But you have to remember that federal races, especially for house seats, while they have a national flavor sometimes, are local races. The base of money that is raised to run these campaigns typically comes first from the home region. But $1 million makes it possible to do things in a race that $200,000 can't buy. I know from experience.

And raising money at home in and of itself becomes exceptionally difficult, especially if an area is economically depressed or if one party or the other has had a difficult time gaining any traction or hope in past elections. In our case, this district is one of the reddest in the nation, by far the reddest in Ohio, designated as R+14 by the Cook Partisan Voting Index (CPVI, R+14 is high!); and no Democrat has held the seat since 1939. Fundraising is difficult, to say the least. Most people do like to support a winner, after all, and convincing anyone, including yourself, that you have a realistic chance of unseating an incumbent like Boehner with his 12 term incumbency and millions in a war chest is excruciatingly compromising, difficult, and challenging.

But we identified this other $1 million campaign, made contact with key figures in it, and got the phone number of the finance director. The campaign had been dormant since the race in 2012; the candidate wasn't running again. So the finance director had moved on to other campaigns, but she still had access to the donor list and the candidate had said that she would share the list with us. But I had to talk with the finance director first and ask for it to get the call list. I didn't know how difficult this would be.

I reached the campaign's former finance director on the phone on Sunday afternoon.

"Hello, this is Tom Poetter. I'm running for congress against Boehner in Ohio's 8th. Ms. X directed me to you to discuss access to her donor list."

"Right ... I'd like to see your campaign prospectus first. Can you send that to me?"

"What's a campaign prospectus? I know sort of by context, but not really."

"Oh my goodness, you don't have a prospectus?" She was really put off and completely unimpressed. She didn't care who I was, what I wanted to do, what I stood for, or that I was running against Boehner.

"Well, I have a website, several policy positions posted there, and some other good writing on who I am and what I want to do with the campaign. Can I send you those materials?"

"No, not necessary. How many phone calls have you made this weekend?"

"None, it's Thanksgiving."

"Do you think Boehner's not making phone calls? He's on the phone right now. He's kicking your butt while you talk to me. You have no idea what you're doing!"

"Maybe, do you want to come work for me, or do you want to help me with this list? Ms. X said we could have the list. I'm asking for it. All you have done is lectured me and you don't even know me."

The conversation deteriorated from there. I couldn't make light of it, or convince her that I was for real. Needless to say, we never got the list.

December 10, 2013

BUTLER COUNTY PROGRESSIVES MEETING, "IT'S ISSUES TIME!"

I was completely upset and disappointed by the bad phone call and the lost list. And call time had trickled to almost no time. My teaching schedule got really busy at the end of the semester, with lots of appointments with students and full days of grading final papers and committee meetings at work. My university position and family were my first priorities. My campaign ran a distant second in terms of priority as the holidays approached.

But the local Oxford Democrats never let up on me. Especially the ones that didn't get invited back to planning meetings. They pressed me at every turn, in public, at church, at other chance meetings, and on email. What they wanted to know was if I was developing "policy chops." Meaning, could I discuss cogently the finer points of representative politics at the local and federal levels? Could I carry on a conversation about all the things that a representative would be up-to-date on?

To prepare for a talk I was asked to give tonight for the Butler County Progressives' quarterly meeting, I started focusing on newspapers, primarily the *New York Times* (which I got every day delivered to the door). I read, and read with interest. I built this new, deeper reading into morning time and late night. I started getting up earlier, about the time Chris left for work at 7 am. I took notes, jotting ideas in a journal, and cutting out pieces that I saved and re-read. I felt like I was making progress. I was learning more than I knew as a regular citizen; as a candidate I was becoming conversant about deficits, free trade agreements, highway bills, sequestration, the affordable care act, foreign relations, defense, jobs, women's health, racial tension, other social issues.

I had been keeping all my notes in one place, so I decided to turn the page and made a list of topics that I could say a few words about in terms of how my campaign would distinguish itself from Boehner's position on the same topics. I tried to focus on things I thought that a representative from a district (not a Speaker of the House) should be conversant about, take a stand on, and push on. I had this neat, hand-written page in my journal already to go. I treated the page like notes for a talk. I hadn't given a scripted talk since the opening rally, and thought that the folks who showed up tonight would want to have a more personal, from the heart and hip intellectual exchange about the issues of the day from a progressive point of view. I wanted them to think I knew stuff and was learning, improving.

Ginger and I showed up a few minutes early for the meeting. Just a few people trickled in. There were the usual suspects, and a few other curious parties. The event had been advertised and I was the keynote speaker. By the time the moderator opened the meeting, about 20 people had taken a seat. I felt incredibly disappointed by the turnout. Like with the rally earlier, I thought that we might draw way more people than we had. I thought maybe 50 people would show tonight, really fill the room and generate a buzz.

The meeting went quickly, the group accomplishing its business in just a few minutes, then, surprisingly, the moderator handed the floor over to a guest who had asked to give an update on the Affordable Care Act. He talked for 45 minutes. I was shocked, dismayed. I barely made it through his talk without having to pee again. I just seethed from head to toe as I sat there smiling. I lost confidence and focus and interest as each minute passed. I felt sure when I stood up to speak that no one would care and would just want the meeting to end. I was more than right about that.

When he finished, the moderator asked Burt to introduce me. Well, we hadn't spoken since we broke up on the car ride back from Springfield a few weeks earlier, but he did an outstanding job. He told a bit about the campaign, its highlights so far, about some of the fun facts in my background and life history, and said, " … Without further ado, I give you the next member of the U.S. House of Representatives from District 8, your candidate, Tom Poetter." It was a really great, rousing introduction. The audience applauded lightly, in no way commensurate with the level of intensity of the introduction.

I made my way to the podium, smiled, and made a self-deprecating joke: "You've heard that line before that you hope the talk is as good as the introduction? (light laughter) I hope I can live up to my billing. Thank you for supporting my run for the U.S. House seat. I wanted to take some time tonight to sketch some ideas for you about ..." And those lines were the highlight of my talk. I stumbled around a few of my notes, left the podium and my notes behind trying to connect with the audience, lost my place, went back to the podium to use my notes, couldn't find them because I had placed them on another table, then in the lull as I searched around the room for my notes a member of the audience blurted out, "What do you make of the new budget deal brokered by Murray and Ryan today?"

I said back, with my eyes bulging wide open with surprise, "I hadn't heard."

She said, "Well, the two reached a deal today ..." and she went on about the situation for five minutes, herself, right in the middle of my talk, stealing the moment and the talk and every last ounce of my soul from me in plain sight. Naked, bare, ignorant.

I blundered around, ended the talk, and in a blurry eyed, angry fit of rage on the way to the car, said to Ginger, "What a disaster. I can't even get a discussion right and the whole evening was a wreck. There is no silver lining in this."

She walked with her head down and like a good soldier said, "It wasn't that bad, Tom. There will be other talks. It'll go better next time." The consummate friend.

At home that night I lamented the hole I had dug for myself. I wanted to quit. I told Chris I could do it without recompense. I could give all the money back we had raised, and there would still be time for someone else to get in the race. She said, "You're not quitting, you're just learning. Hang in there, you'll get it." I thought she would let me off the hook, but she wouldn't. If even Chris wouldn't let me quit, I couldn't quit.

REMODELING

For the next few days, Ginger and I spent some time together debriefing the botched speech, and focusing on the project of landing office space for the campaign.

I made an all out push with friends I knew around town with property to help us find a place. While most of those queries came up dry, several leads looked promising. One large, very prominent office space uptown had housed Planned Parenthood for many years. It was over 2,000 square feet of space, and the owner had gotten $2,000 per month from the Obama campaign in 2012. She wanted the same from me. I made a counter offer, and she rejected it. Right across the street a local landlord had just released a retired beautician from her lease. When we looked at the place, the owner said he didn't have time to remove the 10 olive colored, ceramic sinks circling the space before a lease date of January 1. He wanted $500 per month, sinks included; still too steep, plus uptown parking would be tight. Then we caught a break.

Just by accident, a random phone conversation led to another connection at another real estate rental company that had just lost a tenant in a very accessible property inside the city limits. The property had plenty of parking. When Ginger and I went to see it, we knew immediately that the space was perfect. The entry was above ground, but it was a walkout entry with the office space in the basement of the building. The main room was long and thin, about 6'x17'. This slim room at the front door would be our hub.

I immediately saw in my imagination a call center with a long countertop for a phone bank installed. In the open area shared by the rest of the building, there was a kitchen with a sink and fridge, a large open area with tables and chairs, a restroom (so key!!!), and several other small office rooms.

When the property owner looked at the space with us, she offered the office to us for $250 per month including utilities. She had charged the previous renter that, and thought it was fair. She accepted another $100 per month for an extra room, and we had a three-room office with electricity, heat, A/C, a restroom, kitchen, and large meeting area for a great price, $350 per month. We even had enough money in the bank at that point to pay off the whole rent for 12 months if we had to. We signed the lease, and they spent the next few weeks painting and sprucing up the place for us for move in on 1.1.14.

One of my financial rules for the campaign was that we would never purchase anything unless we had the money. I couldn't live with the specter of debt in the campaign. So, we only rented the place at a price that would allow us to fold the campaign and pay off all our debts at a moment's notice. I wouldn't be saddled with any debt from this effort, a promise I made to myself as well as to Chris. This would change a little bit as we got closer to heavier campaign activity in the late Summer and Fall of 2014 when our output of money increased with the fervor of the campaign, especially for communications and staff salaries. But the same rule always applied: We only buy what we can pay for with existing funds.

Just a few days later I talked my friend Danny Sens into building a countertop in the front office room for a call center. A builder, Danny's son and my son Mitch had played sports together all through their youth and went to high school together. We had become good friends, and he had done a great deal of remodeling work in our home over the years. He agreed to help me but said, "Don't tell anyone I helped you, it might be bad for business." He was only half joking with that sheepish grin of his. "I promise," I said.

So after a busy and exhausting day at work for him, just a week before Christmas, we cased the place at 6 pm, made a tentative plan, drove to Hamilton in his truck, picked out some affordable countertops, bought all the fittings and hardware and wood we would need, and drove back. Danny started cutting and building around 8 pm and we were done at 10 pm. We laughed and talked and worked in a boisterous symbiosis that reflected our long relationship and affection for each other, as well as his interest in what I was doing with the campaign. As a Republican, he would never have donated money to the campaign or knocked on doors for me. In the past, we had gotten into long arguments that spread over several months about taxation. I had argued yes for bonds and levies to support our public schools. He said we were overtaxed, the buildings were good enough, and teachers made plenty of money. We always argued, the levies came and went.

But he would give me more than money; he would be my friend, build a countertop, vote for me, and call to tell me that my uptown campaign sign spelled my name wrong just to keep me loose. Late in the campaign, in September of 2014, Danny and I would take our two sons for lunch right at the beginning of school. The goal was to support them, and just to connect with them as they made their way through their second year of college as roommates. We were so proud of them, and wanted them to know how much we cared for them. That meal was a lot of fun. And we repeated it a few weeks later with a pizza night at their place for the opening of Thursday night football. Just a few months later, Danny would die suddenly of a heart attack on the way to work to build another house, or install another countertop. I wish I could have back all the months I spent on his campaign and trade them in for another night out with Danny.

My best friend, Danny Sens, built my campaign countertop, with love and care.

January 2, 2014
Move-In Day

I scrounged around the house for office items that could go to our new headquarters. I bought a few long, black tables; a small fridge for water and sodas; some office supplies to get started, along with some food and drinks. I found a few chairs and tables to fill in the blanks, along with a dry erase board, some tape and markers and pens and paper and such. I bought a printer/copier (which we would replace several times in a year) and some extension cords, etc.

I hauled it all to HQ and began setting things up. I liked doing that, but saw that there were many imperfections in the space that could be improved. Several areas and doors needed a change of color, they just didn't match and distracted some people, especially Ginger. These areas never got painted. I hung our "Poetter for Congress" banner across a long length of the front room. It remained up for the duration of the campaign unless it traveled to an event.

At work, we experienced our first Winter Term in January. The first three weeks of January constituted a new "semester" in which students could take online and face-to-face classes at Miami in a three-week period. Many faculty did study-abroad workshops and offered courses that students needed online. It created a situation where I didn't have to be back at work teaching classes until late January. This gave me some time and flexibility for running the campaign that I needed and welcomed. I was still responsible as graduate studies director for my department to host interviews for 20 candidates for our doctoral program in January and to make decisions on admission with our committee. This proved to be work that got done mostly on interview dates (Fridays in January) and into February. I prepared for my classes that would start in late January and felt comfortable doing this. It would be the first full semester of campaigning and working at the same time.

I spent considerable time on the phone talking with a local cable company about internet service. County operatives kept telling me that I should be pursuing installation of a call bank that ran with Voice Over Internet Protocol (VOIP). I would need some old, donated computers, head gear for the users, the right software that I could get from a campaign company that supplied and installed this type of program (at a rather steep price, in my opinion), a very robust internet line (probably at least a T-1 Line) with very strong upload capability to handle the call center. I would need an excellent, commercial grade router, too.

As I worked through the local vendors, I found out that only one internet provider in the region could deliver the type of service we thought we needed at our location. The other companies didn't have access to the wiring or had no agreement with existing providers to give us what we wanted. I spent hours on the phone trying to get this figured out. I thought to myself, "It just can't be this hard." It was.

Ultimately, I got a final price from the only vendor who could provide the type of service we thought we needed, a T-1 Line with tremendous uploading capability: $465 per month. That was more than $100 higher than our rent. As I pondered the time it took me to get into a position to get this all set up, I thought of the wasted time, and the lack of action in the campaign. I pulled the trigger and ordered the service. But then it took weeks to get it set up. And when the vendor was on site, the workers said it was a piece of cake to make the router work with the signal. Bill, who came infrequently to Oxford to help out but still carried the title of "Political Director" and supplied the research power behind our initial call lists, said that he could set it up. By the time we had reached mid-February, Bill had failed at hooking up the internet, getting the routers working, etc. We had no internet in the building for more than six weeks after the actual line was installed. Needless to say, we didn't make much progress on putting together a call center in that time period.

But, on a snowy day after the New Year, the office started to hum. Ginger came in and we worked in the office getting it ready. Bill came in and got set up to work there, even without the internet. And Marvin and

I ran call time at Danny's counter. We raised a little bit of money that day, and felt like we were running a campaign. To be honest, the holiday period from mid December to early January is a slow time for campaigning. In Ohio, the weather can be frigid, which it was, and people are committed to family and friends, not to campaigns, necessarily. I know that our campaign "friend" who withheld the call list didn't think it so, but I couldn't imagine taking significant time away from family to spin my wheels on the campaign.

About this time, I learned from Ginger that her father had become ill. In the next few weeks, she would see me through my brightest moment to date in the campaign, a nice comeback from the December 10th debacle, and then quickly quit the campaign for good due to her father's deteriorating health. I really did think that the last three standing so far would be the ones to see my through the campaign. Ginger, my campaign manager. Bill, my political director. And Marvin, my finance director and jack of all trades. None of them would make it to the finish line. My political family would rise like a phoenix out of the ashes. But the smoldering embers would linger for a long time.

January 14, 2014
House Party!

In mid December, friend and local Democrat Janet Lavelle volunteered to host the first, real fundraising house party for the campaign in Oxford. I was grateful for the offer, but didn't know if we could get enough people there to make a difference, if they would have any money to give to politicians after the holidays, and/or if I were up to giving a solid talk. But I had enough distance since the December disaster with the progressives and a growing sense of my feelings, positions, and knowledge regarding the most pressing issues at hand to accept the invitation. I accepted their kind offer and the plans for it came together quickly, nicely. It would be the first good fundraising effort besides our opening week and the initial, spotty calling we had been doing.

As the house party date approached, we found out that Ginger's father was now very ill, with a life-threatening condition. Ginger had begun telling me that she would have to back away from the campaign if things got worse for her dad, and they did. The house party at Janet's proved to be her last campaign event. Ginger and Bill and Marvin called friends and neighbors and tried to pin them down to attend. It's one thing to put out a Facebook post that you are inviting so and so and all of these people to a fundraiser and for them to actually commit to coming to it and to bringing a check. But we reached about 30 rsvps of yes and that felt good. More than 40 people actually filled the house.

I grew increasingly nervous as the event approached, but on the evening of the party, I actually grew calmer. One of my friends at the event came up to me and said, "Just relax, you are great. This is going to be a fantastic event." I didn't feel more pressure, but relief. I appreciated her faith in me. Few people over the course of the first months of the campaign ever said anything like that to me. And people need encouragement sometimes, even if you act like you don't. I definitely needed it.

When the time came for me to talk, over 40 people had jammed into Janet's house. So many cars were parked out front that people had to help with parking outside and to help some older guests to the door. Everyone put in such a great effort, working the greeting table, collecting checks, serving food, and talking it up. I was so proud. Now it felt like we were making progress. When it came time to speak, Ginger gave a really nice introduction, her last official act of the campaign.

And I was off. Introductorily, I told a story that I told many times in short talks about my mom and her faith in my campaign. Suffering from advancing dementia now, she still had moments of clarity periodically. After unnecessarily obsessing about my effort on her behalf (or lack thereof from her perspective) to fill out her annual Publisher's Clearinghouse Sweepstakes entry, she said to me on the phone, "Tom, I think this is going to be a big year. I'm going to win Publisher's Clearinghouse, and you're going to beat Boehner!" That always got a huge round of applause and some laughter, since many people knew my mom and could see and feel that spark in her comment despite her failing health. And then I attacked Boehner on his lack of leadership on a national level, and lack of attention to detail in serving those in his home district, and especially on our differences on income disparity, jobs, healthcare, education, immigration, the Farm Bill (especially cutting food stamps), sequestration, the government shutdown, and the assault on women, from health care to the glass ceiling.

I talked about the issues, and did it somewhat skillfully. I drew out points, and gave examples. I said what I would hope to do in the job, specifically, to address the gaps at hand. I got some laughter, and applause, and their complete attention. I spoke for about 20 minutes, and then Bill was supposed to moderate the q/a. He did, but after the second or third question, he asked to take one, and I agreed, yielding the floor. Then Bill launched into a long, undisciplined tirade about healthcare. I knew that was the end of the campaign for him. He so desperately wanted to be in charge, and to have a voice, and to be recognized, that he couldn't let me have the moment completely. He only lasted another month.

I got the floor back, with little damage done, said thank you and good-night, and talked and mingled for another hour. It was exhilarating.

We made over $2,000 at the party. I was a little disappointed at the amount, thinking that with almost 50 donors there that we might make more than $3,000. But it was the best thing we had done to date and I was pleased. One guest was Jack Stone, whom I had called just that week on the phone about a donation. He had said "no" on the phone to making a donation. I walked up to him and introduced myself and thanked him for coming out and for making a contribution to the campaign. He said, "I didn't write you a check, I just came for the food." And then he walked away.

I actually laughed out loud, and thought, "Wow! So this is how it's going to be?"

If you don't laugh, all you can do is cry. Truth is, every single corner I turned in this campaign I met another Jack Stone.

WINTER
LUNCHEONS
AND COFFEE

We learned in late December 2013 that Matt Guyette out of Greenville, Ohio (Darke County), would be an official challenger in the primary in May 2014. Matt pulled the papers, got the signatures (50 total), and filed for the primary. He was certified by the board of elections, as was I. The campaign team and I didn't take Matt very seriously from the beginning. After all, his full-time job was as a tour guide at the capitol building in DC. He didn't really even live in Greenville anymore. But in Ohio congressional races, you don't even have to live in the district. You just have to get the signatures, and you can appear on the primary ballot. We couldn't discover much of a digital footprint on Guyette, either. No matter, we didn't think he could organize like we could and he didn't live in Butler County, home of Oxford, like we did; the county contains more than 50% of the voting population among six counties, and most of the Democrats.

And we certainly didn't want to spend any time or money trying to beat another Democrat. This would prove to be a near fatal mistake for the campaign. But even in retrospect, I wouldn't do much differently, given the time I had and our staffing.

Before Ginger finally quit the campaign, we had one of our Friday late morning lunch/breakfasts at a local Oxford eatery. It had become routine for us to meet every Friday, to check in, plan, share information. Before we parted for the last time as campaign colleagues, we talked about Guyette and what we had to do to beat him.

"Breathe," Ginger said. And we laughed and parted as friends.

Over that January period, I met with several possible, local donors. I want to share what the meetings were like, and how differently things could go in these types of situations.

The first meeting I had was with a friend/colleague from Miami. He had some political background and he was surprised I decided to run. I would describe him as skeptical, even after I had been in the race a couple of months and some history was starting to build about my campaign in the papers, at events, online. We had lunch at a local eatery, and he quizzed me about my plans. Almost everything I said made him cringe.

After one cringe, I finally said, "What's wrong with that?"

"You can't get elected saying that."

"So you think I can get elected saying the 'right' things?"

"No."

We laughed. I said, "Then I'm not going to pretend to be someone I'm not to win a few thousand more votes and lose by 35% rather than 40%. That's not in the cards for me. I'm just not that kind of person. Of course, I'm running in this campaign to win, and to compete. But I know, and you know, and Boehner knows that I can't win."

We talked a few more minutes, and parted as friends. I asked him many times for a campaign contribution, and he never came through. We haven't spoken since.

Another meeting was with a prominent church member, who happened to be a Republican, and his wife, who happened to be a Democrat. We met for late morning coffee, and we discussed some church projects as we warmed up. Then we talked politics, bantering and enjoying the conversation. After a few minutes, my friend reached in his pocket while his wife smiled, pulled out a bill, and reached under the table. I reached out my hand, feeling very awkward, and took the money. I'll never forget that I took it "under the table." I laughed and said, "This is very kind. It's the first $100 bill I've seen in a long time. And it's the limit of what I can take in cash. I have to hand this to my treasurer later today, and you'll get a receipt and a thank you note for the money. It's very generous. Thank you."

As we shook hands and prepared to part ways, he said, "There's more where that came from." And later when I asked, he sent me a large check with a nice note about the campaign's progress.

At another meeting, I met a prominent Oxford citizen with an interest in politics. I knew members of his family well, and he had always been a key figure in significant town events, moving the ball when talks stalled, fueling the fire with a donation, rallying friends, etc. I asked him for a sizeable donation. He had the money. He could spare it, and had given prominently to other candidates in the past. He liked me, I knew that then and know that now, and I received a check from him for $250 a week later, after I followed up with a phone call. But he never repeated the gift, after many requests. Like many potential donors who could have helped push me into a situation where I could have bought media late in the race, he couldn't, wouldn't take that next step of really investing in me. After all this time, this very clear fact, to me, stings. He gave me $250. But it should have been $2,500. And if 10 more people would have, who could have and should have given me $2,500, we could have mounted a much more effective and ground-breaking campaign, especially in the media late in the race, when we were hamstrung for funds. I'm thankful for the contribution, and bitter about it, all at the same time. Can you blame me?

January 22, 2014
DARKE COUNTY DEMOCRATIC PARTY ENDORSEMENT MEETING

It snowed like crazy, practically a blizzard, this evening. But I never heard a word from the Darke County Democratic Committee that the meeting to endorse candidates for the 2014 races would be canceled and I couldn't reach the chair by phone. They had no online presence, so there was no way to find any kind of posted announcement about cancelation on Facebook or a website. My best guess was that the meeting would be canceled. But I got in the Acadia and took off by myself on the 60-mile trek to Greenville. I knew I was late, but I couldn't help it, the roads were terrible and I just crawled along. I finally found my way to the meeting place, but it was so hard to find that I almost gave up. It was in a darkened building, and the shades had been drawn so you couldn't even tell which room was lighted for a meeting. When I got there, I barged in, and had to awkwardly introduce myself, shaking off the snow from my coat and cold snot from my nose. The 15 members gathered there graciously pulled up a chair for me and I settled in for the meeting, as they continued.

And the meeting dragged on. By the time they got to the endorsement of candidates, only one other candidate—running for state senate in the district—had shown up. We had actually met at several early campaign events in Miami County, and I liked her, pledged her my support: I would work with her in any way our campaigns saw fit.

When the time came, the members asked her to give the first pitch. They listened to her as she spoke, just briefly about her race and why she was getting into it. She had served previously as mayor of a small city in Miami County, neighboring Darke, and her husband had been longtime chair of the county's party. Members got into a long discussion then about how there was another person running for the seat and how they didn't see how they could endorse someone before the primary. While they argued and stalled, the chair stopped the whole thing and said, "Why don't we hear from Mr. Poetter now?"

So I stood up and thanked the group for inviting me, then I launched into Boehner. The group liked my short talk, which I was perfecting with practice under the gun, and gave me a unanimous endorsement and pledged their support no matter what.

I took a few questions and the first person asked, "How old are you?"

"51."

"No way. You're not a day over 35."

"No sir! I'm 51. But thanks for the compliment, I think! I traveled this part of the state my whole life including during the blizzard of '78 as a teenager. And tonight's drive here reminded me a lot of those days."

That got a good laugh, and the members loved that, and then I said, "Well, you know, like the future state senator here, I am going to be contested by Matt Guyette in the primary, who hails from right here in Greenville." The entire room looked shocked. They had never heard of Guyette, and said that if he couldn't make it to the endorsement meeting in his own "hometown" that he wasn't worth it anyway. Then I said, "Well, the future state senator made it here, and you won't endorse her for a contested primary."

Then a member said, "Poetter's right. I move we endorse Dee Gillis for State Senate."

"I second that."

Then the chair said, "Okay, well ... All those in favor?"

"Aye," the room clamored.

The two snow warriors got endorsed that night. I couldn't have been happier.

The fact of the matter was that there were next to no votes in Darke County for a Democrat, especially one running against Boehner. And I received maybe a total of $250 from Darke County for the race. The party gave me nothing. Only a few citizens chipped in begrudgingly. In the room that night was a person who had given generously to candidates all over the state, and to people who had run for the congressional seat against Boehner in the past. I had already called her once, and she said she wouldn't give. That night after greeting her for the first time face-to-face, I asked again.

"Tom, it's not that I don't like you. I think you'll be a great candidate. But you can't win. And I'm always so disappointed in the results that I just can't put my money in that race anymore. I'm sorry." She was gracious, though wrong; I didn't argue with her.

But it's the moment when I understood the difference between those who understood what running meant to us AND donors/party members like her. She thought politics was about winning, and investing in seats that could be gotten. Maybe there is something smart about that. But we were running as a service, as a way for views to be heard, so the forgotten Democratic minority in District 8 could have a voice, even if only for a few short months, and to have someone to vote for in the election. No more uncontested races, no matter the score.

I called her five more times in the next months. No. No. No. No. No.

She could have really helped us and didn't. Darke County could have helped us, but didn't. They have few members, little infrastructure, and few elected officials to push things forward. A complete, total dead end in the snow, but I had their endorsement.

January 23, 2014

HOUSE PARTY 2

We were so excited to be invited for another house party in a neighboring city, a Republican stronghold with a few Democrats. People had heard of our successful party in Oxford and an eager party member—someone known in Democratic circles as being particularly boisterous on Facebook—had invited us to his home and promised a good turnout of people eager to hear from the person from Oxford who would unseat Boehner. We spoke on the phone cordially and I agreed to the event. I "routinely" asked (it was only our second house party!) that he help us set up a staff member at the door at a table in order to greet people and to take contributions and give receipts, but he balked.

"No one is going to give you money from this group until they meet you."

I was shocked, but I said, "I'm going to be the nominee. There isn't anyone else in this race who can even compete with Boehner. I could really use everyone's upfront support. That's how these house party things work."

"Not in our town. Give a good talk and you'll do fine."

I was skeptical and extremely put off, but I decided to keep the date. I thought, "When in Rome."

It turned out to be one of the coldest nights of the year. But people came, and the party turned fun, with people interacting and laughing and eating and drinking. The host and his wife were great, very cordial, welcoming, happy to have us. When it came time for me to give my talk, the group had already been warmed up by Bill and Gerald, Bill's friend who had attended our opening night event in Oxford, was still in school, and supported our work when time allowed. My talk went well, it was more natural and flowing and I was less tied to my notes, now. But the q/a was a little weird, with people in attendance taking strong stands for issues they believed in, held firm positions on, and really pressed me on these areas for my views. Then I realized as I was talking that the citizens gathered really didn't care about my views, but mainly cared about voicing their own and being heard. Okay. I listened to them, responded, but I realized in the moment that my speak back wasn't usually strong enough for them and I could sense that a few of the attendees were unhappy with that. But overall it went very well.

A few checks trickled in by the end of the night, which got handed to Bill as people left the party. But it was only a few hundred dollars total, just awful for such a great event and so discouraging. With about 30 people there, each giving $50 or $100 minimum, we should have made $2,000. I froze my butt off in the street without a jacket afterward talking with a supporter. It was worth it that night. But the list of attendees, which we cultivated at the event and then called and wrote to continually throughout the campaign, hardly came through for us financially, let alone as volunteers to knock on doors or attend other events. Perhaps I earned their vote that night. But I found out something very interesting about the pockets of party members throughout Butler County and the rest of the district. Many Democrats I met would vote, in both the primary and general elections, but they wouldn't "help."

Meaning, they did not construe their civic duty to the party in terms of actually working on a campaign or donating to it financially. Later in the campaign these party members/supporters became known pejoratively as "Facebook" Democrats. They think that campaigns are about Facebook posts. But they aren't. Facebook has its place, but campaigns are still waged face to face, and in the "real" media, on radio and TV, where name recognition and influence can be gained. And money does matter. I couldn't hire a staff because we had no money. Volunteers had carried everything to this point. Everyone working on the campaign volunteered his or her time and efforts. But this volunteer approach, while quaint, has its limits, especially when you are running against a monster like the Boehner machine.

Facebook doesn't pay the bills, or even reach voters who don't have the internet or hate online media (many do). I also found out over the course of the campaign that the host of what became known as the "Icicle Party"—named for the freezing weather and the monetary freeze out—would never make a campaign contribution. He expected a quid pro quo relationship, wherein the campaign would avail itself of certain services he could provide for the campaign on a commercial basis. When we decided we couldn't go with his non-union goods, he froze us out. Our Democratic friend held a house party for us to help his own business and never gave a single dollar to the campaign when we didn't scratch his back.

Democratic truth at its epitome. A hard lesson. A bitter pill.

January 30, 2014

BUTLER COUNTY DEMOCRATIC PARTY ENDORSEMENT MEETING

I should have been ready for this event, but I wasn't. I realized that night that I really didn't have this all together, after a busy day working with students and teaching and after driving over to Hamilton for the event in another snowstorm. I thought the event was to be held at Democratic Party Headquarters at 7 pm, but I had the wrong venue. I sat in the parking lot of headquarters for about 15 minutes in a raging snowstorm. I thought I was just early. I called a friend who I knew would be at the county party meeting and he left the actual meeting to take my call and whisper-screamed, "Where are you?" I said I was at headquarters and he informed me that I was almost an hour late and I thought I was an hour early! The meeting started at 6 pm! And I had to drive all the way across town to the venue just to get there more than an hour late. I barely made it in and out of the parking lot without getting stuck in the snow. I chugged over there and when I walked in, there sat Matt Guyette, my primary competitor, waiting in the lobby. I introduced myself, and he said, "I think we're up next. I've been here awhile."

"Great," I said, and we made some small talk after I went to the restroom. His girlfriend was his campaign manager, and now he was ahead of me on staff. With Ginger out, and Bill really not in tune enough to even make an effort to replace her (if he really wanted to be my campaign manager he would have been prepping me for this event, at least keeping me from being late!),

I basically only had Marv working on the campaign consistently with me. I asked Matt point blank, "When you realized I was in the race and that you couldn't beat me with Butler County in my back pocket, why did you file?"

"I've always wanted to run for congress. It's my chance to do it."

"We're kindred spirits in that regard, I guess, in terms of seeing our chance and taking it."

And then the chair called us back. They took us into the executive committee session one at a time. They asked me to give my elevator speech. I did that. They asked me a few questions and it was very cordial. They basically said I had the endorsement wrapped up, no matter what Guyette did, since it was already in the meeting's agenda, "Approve candidate endorsements in 2014 races: Tom Poetter, U.S. House District 8."

I thought that I was off the hook then, but then when the meeting started, with about 150 people present in the auditorium from all over the county, the chair announced from the podium that each candidate would have two minutes to speak to the audience. I did my speech again, though I was tired and it fell sort of flat. This all happened after I was endorsed, and to be honest, I thought Guyette gave a better talk than I did. At one point while listening to him I wished I could just quit and let him do it. And I could have done that in that moment and just walked away. Believe me, it crossed my mind. But I didn't do it …

Then the Butler County Chair gave her pitch for a spring push for the local party. It was all built around one race that the party thought it could compete in. I was somewhat shocked, especially as the chair talked about how they planned to put people to work on this one race, how they wanted to raise money for this one race, and how they wanted to spend it to win this one race. "What about our race?" I screamed out in my head. And I should have been screaming. From this moment on the county did next to nothing to support my race. They gave me no money. They recruited few volunteers. They extended no publicity. They left that all to me, and then later the party wanted to draw on our resources to help *them* and their local candidate out! It didn't feel like a team effort. The party asked everything of me and the party delivered nothing, except a hollow, relatively meaningless endorsement.

But I was thrilled at the time to have the county's endorsement. I couldn't imagine going on without it. But I found out quickly that it meant next to nothing in terms of generating votes in the primary or general election campaigns. Maybe it was instrumental in helping me win the primary, in a way. But the set up was complete, and devastating. I thought from the beginning that the county party existed to help Democrats running for office. I found that in our case it was just the opposite; local Democrats thought my campaign existed to help them! The county expected us to have success, especially financial success, and then to share that success down the ladder with other local candidates. I was totally confused and would remain this way throughout the campaign. Everything looked upside down, backwards, sideways at every turn.

If I knew then what I know now, I would have just walked away that night and let Matt Guyette run unopposed. I could have dropped out. But going back to the beginning, Chris wouldn't let me drop out in the first month. Now I was several months in. There was nowhere to go but even further down this rabbit hole.

Early February, 2014

WINTER DOLDRUMS TAKE HOLD OF A WITHERING CAMPAIGN

There is no secret here, our campaign floundered after the Butler County endorsement, even if just for a week. So much can happen in a week!

I had lost Ginger, my campaign manager, for good. Bill paid less and less attention to the campaign, almost completely stopped coming to Oxford to work at headquarters, and failed on his attempts to provide us with the type of call lists of donors that we needed to raise serious money. He had no relationship to the state/county party members who could help us. Bill? A dead end.

The only person I had left that I could count on was Marv. He came in religiously to run call time with me. We made about 75 calls a night, and we talked, and he kept my spirits and hopes up every day. What a blessing he was in these dark hours and days, when the snow fell deep, making it hard to even get to the office. We had very little success on the phone, but we plugged away at it and we kept each other in good spirits.

Chris and I acted like strangers in the night. I was home so little. She left for work at 7:00 am and got home around 5:30 pm. I often had call time or an event in the evening. We barely saw each other, and when we did, we bickered and fought. The weather was terrible and depressing, each day was a slog without marital support. She felt I had checked out of the marriage to run a campaign. I felt she had checked out of the marriage because I was running a campaign that she wouldn't let me quit. Bitterness abounded. The only respite we had came when we could disappear on the road to watch Sam play hockey with his high school team. But when we were on the road, all anyone wanted to talk about was the campaign. Ugly.

To boot, we faced our first serious filing deadline with the Federal Election Commission (FEC) and it would have to be done electronically. The person who signed on early as a placeholder in the treasurer's position balked at continuing given the ominous tasks ahead in terms of filing the financial information of the campaign, so I had to scramble. I narrowed the list to one person, a friend who worked in accounting. I begged her to help me; she agreed to do it for free because of our friendship and because she liked my spirit, if not the campaign itself or my politics. What a Godsend she turned out to be, seeing us through all the morass of paperwork and rules and money problems that even a small campaign like ours encounters when running for federal office.

I knew, overall, that something had to give. Marv and I couldn't run the campaign ourselves. While my confidence grew in public meetings—I had a very good recent performance at an event with the Butler County Progressives who asked me to be the undercard for Nina Turner, one of the state's only African American state senators and a star on national TV talk shows running for Secretary of State—I didn't have anyone working with us to plan events or to work on short and long-term strategies for increasing our voter contact, for canvassing, for using the Democratic voter database, for fundraising, etc. But Marv and I had begun to talk seriously about what we needed to do. Things had to change, quickly.

We decided I had to reach out for help. I called the Butler County Chair, told her our issues with fundraising and with a lack of personnel, and she encouraged me to call the Chair of the State party and she herself gave me a few names of locals who might consider being my campaign manager, which I tucked in my back pocket. I called the State Chair, and he was so gracious, taking my call and volunteering to meet the county chair and me in Dayton for a meeting that Thursday. He would bring his head of campaign finance and we could hash out a way forward. I felt so valued and hopeful after that call. I quickly set up the meeting, and would drive the county chair up for it.

In the meantime, Bill and his friend, Gerald, who would actually wind up playing a major role in the campaign later, attended a Butler County campaign workshop with me on February 6 at the party's headquarters. The meeting had already been canceled twice for snowy weather. So the operatives announced that the meeting would happen on the third try no matter the weather, and the weather was awful. But we showed up and heard more about campaign finance and running a campaign from two old friends I hadn't seen since the blow up meeting at my house in October, Max Smith and Cindy Winter. The meeting would prove to be helpful, and underscore Bill's growing distance. Something definitely had to change with him. Either I needed to promote him or cut him loose.

One of the great outcomes of the workshop came during the practice sessions all of the candidates there participated in during the last hour. Each of us gave our elevator speeches and the county operatives critiqued them on the spot. I went first since I had the most experience so far and nailed it. Others floundered and sputtered, just trying to get it together. This helped me confidence wise, and it didn't hurt that several people there saw me and pledged their support. Several of them made campaign contributions on the spot. One new friend who attended the session as a first time candidate from the Cleveland area handed me $60 in cash for gas money. I said, "You have a much longer way to drive. Please, keep it." He said, "Son, you're running against Boehner. Take it." I did.

DAYTON MEETING
WITH THE
STATE CHAIR

The Butler County chair, Nicole Mantle, drove up with me to Dayton to meet with the state chair, Chris Redfern, and the state's Democratic director of finance, Erik Greathouse. We met at a restaurant and had some small talk before ordering. I got to speak directly with the state chair while we brainstormed for about 15 minutes straight, while Erik and Nicole spoke together for a while. Mr. Redfern and I hadn't met before, just talked on the phone, and he wanted to hear my story first hand, how I got into this race, what motivated me, what I wanted to accomplish. He liked me, I could tell after a couple of minutes, and offered to help by giving me greater access to donor lists to be supplied by Mr. Greathouse. He wanted to know if I could come to Columbus or the next day for a meeting to get this going. No time to waste.

I said, "I can't. I have appointments with students and teach class tomorrow night. I can't do it. But I can meet next Tuesday."

He said, pointedly, "It doesn't seem like you're that serious about running."

I said, "Of course, I'm serious. I'm sitting right here, and I shouldn't even be here. I'm busy. I have a job. I'm good at it and that's my first priority. And the time I'm spending on the campaign ... I'm not spending with my family. This is a huge step for me, and I have to put myself in a position to win a primary before even taking the next step running against a behemoth. We need money and a staff and your help. Are you going to help me?"

He softened, liked my spunk, "Yes, we are going to help you. You set up a meeting with Erik for as soon as possible and he'll get you everything you need to get a good start."

I asked, "How much money do you think I can raise if I really work at it?"

Chris said, "You need at least $1 million to have any chance. But you can't raise even $100,000 in this short of time. You shoot for $100,000; getting there would even be impressive."

"What you really need," he continued, "is a personal assistant. You can pay that person $10 an hour to help you organize your work. The person doesn't even have to be experienced. That's a good use of some of your early money and you'll make it back quickly as you start raising money on the phone and online. But without a campaign manager, that will help you. And we will do all of the paper work for the employee at the state level, pay all the taxes and health insurance for your employee so you don't have to set up any kind of infrastructure for them. That's too much work, and we have that already in place. It's something we can give you that no one else can."

I appreciated the offer of support, and it really did help to have some official input from the higher ups about the state of our campaign and what we needed to do. I continued to ask a few questions, which Erik and Chris fielded. The most important one, "Don't I need a campaign manager?"

Without hesitation, Erik offered, "Tom, you can run this campaign, obviously. But you can't do finance. It's a particular skill, it takes experience, and it takes time. You need a finance director more than anything else. We understand that Marv is helping you, but you need a pro. The most important thing for us to do is to get you a finance director."

I nodded, and smiled. And we were on our way home after cordial, very friendly goodbyes. I had two new friends. That wouldn't change through the end of the campaign.

On the way home in the car, Nicole felt like we had made progress. I had set up the meeting with Erik for the next week. She couldn't go with me, but that was okay. At this point, I needed to leave the county apparatus behind anyway. It couldn't yield help with fundraising. It couldn't find me the personnel or the volunteers I needed. This week would mark the last cordial meetings that Nicole and I would have. Later we would fall out over money, of course.

I can't say how much this meeting meant to me. To have Chris and Erik take an interest in our long-shot campaign meant a great deal. Of course, knowing what we know now, with all of the criticism about the lack of good candidates for federal positions in this 2014 pool and their complete lack of success, and the debacle with the governor candidate, pulling down all of the other tremendous statewide candidates, Erik and Chris wouldn't survive 2014 with their positions. But on this one occasion, to me, they showed leadership, and expertise, and care. I feel sorry for their losses during the 2014 campaigns. I think they tried their best, perhaps made quite a few mistakes, and paid for them dearly with their jobs and positions. This, I learned, was the name of the game. Win, or put up a good fight and a show, or you're out. They were out.

Part One—
Dayton-Celina
Circuit

Marv is retired, so he had time to spare on the campaign. When we got the meeting set up with the state party's finance director to discuss the campaigns next steps with finance, Marv is the only person I didn't mind driving me. A terrific driver, and friend. We set it up so that we would be in Dayton by 2 pm and then in Celina for the Mercer County Democratic Party endorsement meeting by 7 pm. This would be a 200-mile trip in the car: exhausting, and exhilarating. When we got to Dayton, we met Erik at a Starbucks near the University of Dayton. We began talking about financing the campaign in three stages of action.

First, we re-visited the topic of my friends and family list and our progress in asking them to support my campaign. How many names did I have? How many people had I asked for support from it so far? Could I build the list with more names? I said I had about 200 names (loosely). I said I had asked about 50 people close to me for money, at least indirectly through email. Most of these attempts had yielded spotty responses. I didn't have a feel yet on the response rate to my list—who was actually supportive or not supportive—who had been asked properly and who had not. This was a huge gap, and one that we had to take immediate action on. Erik said we had to make a strong, immediate commitment to asking everyone I knew to support my campaign with a substantive donation. Both Marv and I understood this line of thought and openly committed to him that we would pursue this part of our campaign finance plan with more vigor and purpose.

Truth be told, I had a tremendous problem with this aspect of the campaign, which I mentioned earlier. Raising money from friends haunted me from the beginning. It was painful to ask people I knew well for money. The bottom line is that I hated the idea of them saying <u>no</u>. From the beginning, I decided NOT to ask certain people because I could not stand the outcome of <u>no</u>. Meaning, I was frightened that <u>no</u> would permanently change our relationship. Of course, <u>no</u> did change my relationship with countless individuals whom I did ask for money. I protected a very, very short list of people from this nemesis. When they read this, they will know who they are because I never asked them for a cent. Some of them gave on their own without being asked, but most did not. We are still friends today. In a very cowardly way, I think, I just could not stand to lose their friendship over this campaign.

I asked many, many other people on my friends and family list to contribute over the life of the campaign. Over the period of time since I started this venture, I have dealt with this in various ways. I have been angry about it, sad, surprised, resigned, and thoroughly disgusted. I have never come to terms with friends and family members who sent me nothing when I asked them directly for help, either through the mail or on the phone. In almost every case I simply wrote them off and haven't spoken with them since. My reasoning is that if you are friends with someone running for congress, or related, how can you not give that person $25? Your politics don't matter. Your immediate feelings don't matter. Differences on issues DO NOT MATTER! If we are friends, kin, you donate. If not, we aren't friends. I am running for congress against an icon no one can stand, on either side! You have to make a donation! I still can't see any way around this position. This position reveals one of the great personal risks of running a campaign—personal loss.

Second, whom were we calling from the lists we did have? What kind of donors populated the lists? How did we keep track of the calls, of the pledges, of our communications? Did we have mailings going out? Did I call the people who received mailings, and vice versa, did people I call get a mailer? Erik pledged that he would cultivate a better, more thorough, and more targeted list of numbers and addresses of Ohio donors ASAP and send it to us, which he did in a matter of days. But we had to have a plan and a system for working with the list, harvesting from it.

And third, what plan of action did we have for moving forward with personnel? Was I interested in finding a new finance director/campaign manager? We discussed many of the in-house options, locals we knew that might be able to help us. All of them seemed to us at the time to be insurmountable dead ends. Then Erik mentioned a friend working with a national group, supporting Democratic campaigns at the federal level, who could consult with us and help us develop a media campaign. But we had to have a finance director, who would probably want to also be the campaign manager, since Ginger had stepped away permanently. We were interested in following up on a lead that Erik had of a person, a close friend of his, who had run campaigns in the past but who hadn't taken on a new campaign yet, and was just waiting for the right call.

Feeling really excited about the potential for taking this to the next level and about getting the kind of help we needed, Marv and I both nodded yes. I said, "We need help. Thanks for opening these doors for us."

Very graciously, Marv agreed that he could help out like he had been doing, but he couldn't run the financial part of the campaign, he just didn't have enough knowledge about what to do. He would step aside if we hired someone new. He wanted to help the campaign and help me get elected. That's all he cared about, and would do whatever it took, including giving way. I appreciated that, and told Marv that on the trip up to Celina. Our first leg had been terrific. We had work to do, but we also had new hope.

February 18, 2014

Part Two— Mercer County Endorsement Meeting, Celina

On the way to Celina from Dayton and our meeting with Erik, we drove through my hometown of St. Marys, only eight miles east of Celina. Growing up, we always viewed Celina as our biggest rival in school sports. We shared the (in)famous Grand Lake St. Marys (famous for its reputation as a family-friendly, high quality lake for boating and fishing that generations of people in Ohio have enjoyed—and infamous for its recent algae bloom caused by agricultural run-off, making the lake largely unusable for recreation and as a result destroying property values), though St. Marys housed the state park and other amenities, like well-populated beaches for swimming and campgrounds. I never knew much about the real Celina, or Mercer County, really, during my youth. I found out a lot more about the county at the endorsement meeting tonight.

Both St. Marys and Celina lie just outside of Ohio's District 8. Celina is the county seat of Mercer County, but only the southern portion of Mercer, excluding Celina, is in District 8. The rest of the district is composed of five other complete counties: Darke, Preble, Miami, Butler, and Clark.

We passed through St. Marys on the way to Celina, and I pointed out some landmarks in my old hometown. Marv humored me, and we made our way to Celina with just a little time to spare. We decided to stop near the railroad tracks on the east side and eat at Casey Jones Steak House. I told Marv that while growing up I had always wanted to stop in there, but my family never would or just never did.

When we entered, the hostesses tried to escort us to the Kiwanis meetings. We had on blazers, so we must have looked the part of guest speakers. I'm sure the Celina Kiwanis wouldn't have liked my spiel much! We said, "No, we're just passing through. Two for dinner." I had never realized that the restaurant featured a buffet, which delighted us! We each got a load of what we wanted, including fried chicken and mashed potatoes. As is the case for many campaign meals, if eaten on the road, they aren't usually of the healthy or low calorie type! Hungry from travel and thinking, we indulged.

We rolled ourselves out of Casey Jones with plenty of time to spare for the meeting, arriving at 6:55 pm. We entered the courthouse where the meeting would be held in a beautiful conference room on the lower level. The beauty of the room struck us, especially the ornate ceilings, remodeled recently to their original condition. And the Mercer County Democrats received us so warmly. The Chair welcomed us first thing at the meeting, saying that the bulk of the business they had would be devoted to hearing me out and deciding on endorsing me or not, throwing me a wink when she said this. Before the meeting, the members, all of them, about 15 total, gave me a personal greeting and congratulated me on running against Boehner. After a few minutes of business items, the chair turned the meeting over to me.

"Tom, please take a few minutes to tell us about yourself and your campaign."

I stood in my place around the tables set up in a horseshoe for the meeting, and let loose.

"I just want you to know how much it means for me to basically come home, to meet all of you, and to be welcomed by all of you. Today has been quite a day of learning for us, Marv and I met with the state party's director of finance in Dayton earlier, and we have a plan for funding this campaign to compete wholeheartedly against the speaker for every vote. And it is a pleasure to be here with you in Mercer County today to ask for your endorsement as the Democratic candidate for the U.S. House of Representatives. Let me say a few words first about growing up in this area, and then a few words about my campaign …"

I did about 15 minutes of free flowing, very natural, and spirited talking about my formative years in the region, my career in education as teacher, coach, and professor, and my recent immersion into politics. At the end of the speech, during which I never used a note, the entire group applauded. I was shocked, and humbled, and so gratified. I thanked them profusely for their support and spirit. Before the meeting, one of the members had said when he first joined the party in the 1970s, Democrats held EVERY political seat in county politics. Now, we held 0, and that it was good to see someone "young" like me continue the good fight against such great odds. I thanked him extensively for his comments and insights and kind words.

At the far end of the table, the senior member of the group stood up before the chair had a chance to intervene and said, "Tom, that's the best speech we've ever heard by a candidate in Mercer County. We want you to know how much we appreciate you running against Boehner. I would like to ask the Chair to invite you out of the room while we deliberate our next steps."

I stood again, thanked the group, and exited the room with Marv. Marv grabbed me by the arm and said, "That was great. Wow!" I agreed, and said, "That's the best I can do, I hope they will endorse tonight." Marv laughed and said, "I can see through the window that they are passing a hat right now. They are going to do more than endorse you tonight."

We both laughed, and the Chair soon invited us in. In front of her was a bag full of $20 bills, and the treasurer had his checkbook out writing us a check for $300. While she talked, the county party treasurer handed Marv the check and the Chair said, "Tom, we want you to have this check as a token of our appreciation. We will donate more throughout the campaign, but we just wanted you to know how much we believe in you and tonight we voted to endorse you for the house race. Also, we would like you to come back to Celina for the annual Democratic Party Ox Roast on April 25. Will you come back and speak again?"

I said, "Yes, of course I will, and I am so thankful and humbled by your support. We really need it and appreciate it. I will be back April 25, and I don't have to headline it, get whomever you can to come as well and I will gladly participate. I'm just glad to have met all of you tonight. It's by far the best night we have had on this campaign. Thank you."

I shook hands with everyone on our way out, as did Marv. Marv and I high-fived at the car, and we talked and planned and dreamed all the way home.

BILL'S WATERLOO

So much happened in the next few days. Time is so compressed in a campaign at times. It might feel like nothing is happening at all for weeks, and then all of a sudden the dominos start falling and the campaign goes crashing ahead, sometimes brilliantly, sometimes haltingly and with jagged edges. Here's how things went down for the campaign in this short time period, just about 48 hours.

For starters, Erik gave me the phone number for Ben Shepherd with The Jackson Team, a political consulting group out of Iowa that made a name for itself working with underdog congressional candidates over the past decades, putting together direct mail campaigns along with other aspects of campaigning including polling, web creation, media support, etc. Erik encouraged me to call Ben, a friend of his, since he had already talked to Ben as a friend and colleague about our campaign and Ben had expressed interest in helping us. This would be a courtesy call he would be giving to me, with the biggest step yet to take being the hiring of a finance director and campaign manager. Nothing else could really happen until we solved the personnel problem. But first steps first … I called Ben.

"Ben, it's Tom Poetter calling from Ohio. How are you?"

"Tom! The giant slayer from District 8. So you think you can beat Boehner?"

"Sure, why not? Isn't he ripe for the picking with all the mess he's caused the nation? The government shutdown? How reckless. And the incredible lack of care he extends here to his own constituents? It's time someone gave him a tough race, all he can handle. But we need help just to run a decent campaign and Erik says you might be able to help us out …"

We spent the next few minutes discussing what The Jackson Team does and what Ben thought he could do for our race. I brought up the idea of him putting together a direct mail fundraising campaign for us. He balked at going there right away, suggesting we had to get a finance director and a campaign manager in place first. If we could get that done, then we could talk.

We hit it off on the phone, and ended things very cordially. Before closing, Ben said, "Erik and I have been talking about Clyde Tate from Florida. He is available, and I am giving him a call today to offer him the job as finance director and campaign manager of your campaign. Do you understand what I'm saying? I'm getting involved in your campaign right now, and you need to trust us with this step. If we can get Clyde to come, you will be all set. We can move ahead. Are you in?"

I thought for a split second. I didn't like anyone ever telling me what to do. I didn't like being beholden to others, especially people I didn't know. But this race would go nowhere without expertise and leadership. We desperately needed someone with more experience than Bill had to enter the campaign and push us ahead. No one locally had stepped in. We didn't think anyone we knew or had met could do it anyway. So I decided on the spot that I liked Ben and that all that he said had impressed me, convincing me to say yes.

"Go for it," I said, as confidently as I could. Then I admitted that I felt cornered a bit, having "outsiders" making such big decisions for our little campaign, but my campaign nonetheless. I felt as though I could basically trust no one, since almost everyone I trusted from the beginning let me down, overshot what they could do, or just flat out lied and cheated me out of time and money, or at least wanted to do so before I stopped them in their tracks or they eliminated themselves!

Ben laughed, "Listen, this is a big deal. I get it. You are a great candidate, I've studied you and I don't take just any candidate on as a client. But you need help and I really can't do anything for you from this distance right now. And Erik can't do more than he's doing right now. You need to let me get Clyde on board with you on location in Ohio, and then we can talk later about next steps on the campaign. You don't owe me anything. We'll wind up doing business later. For now, I assure you, this is a good step."

"You bet," I said, and thanked him profusely.

Over the next day I agonized, waiting for Ben to call back. He didn't. And like the undisciplined suitor hoping for a call back from the damsel, I dialed Ben's number a few times without actually calling. Instead, I called a meeting in Oxford with Ben and Marv. I wanted them to know how this was all going down, to get their input, support.

When we met that night, both Marv and Bill acted like they agreed with the direction things had begun to tilt, in particular, offering an outsider a paid position as finance director/campaign manager. Marv wanted help, and agreed to step aside if necessary, and I assured Bill that his position would remain in tact as political director—running the website, helping with research, and feeding me issues and angles and ideas—and that I would do everything I could to make his position a paid position once someone came in to put us on track in terms of leadership. They both agreed, acted amiably enough, and we all parted that night on good terms. Both of them stated that we needed an influx of talent and that they welcomed it.

The next morning I had an email message from Bill in my in box. I figured he had written to me about our next meeting. Nope. It was an ultimatum letter. He wanted to know: How did I think he would just settle for an outsider coming in? He felt that he should have already been promoted to a paid position as campaign manager, and that he felt shorted and under-appreciated. It was a long, devastating harangue that permanently ended my respect for Bill. But I felt as though we needed him, and I wrote a conciliatory note back, but didn't move from the position of pursuing Clyde Tate.

He wrote back that it was all or nothing. "It's me or Clyde Tate."

I wrote back, "It's Clyde Tate."

Here lies Bill Higby: Dead to me, dead to our campaign.

I wanted him to continue. He gave an ultimatum. Devastating. BUT, out of the fire, iron.

LETTERS,
LETTERS, LETTERS

With Bill out now permanently, I turned my attention to raising money from my friends/family list and to hiring a finance director/campaign manager. The now typical day went like this, if there wasn't an event planned: I worked all day at my job, then after Marv and I worked the phones in the evening, I retreated to my home, spent some time with Chris, and then stayed up after she went to bed and wrote letters to friends and family asking for a campaign donation. I did the letter writing systematically, now adding names to my list, building a spreadsheet, and keeping track of responses. I decided not to send out a generic letter with a return envelope. I had already tried generic email and social media pleas with very little return. Instead, I wrote a hand written note to each person or family member requesting a certain amount of money. I included a self addressed, stamped envelope (SASE). We had some note cards with envelopes made up with our campaign logo used mostly for thank you notes. We ordered 2,000+ and got a great deal. I used them for this letter-writing project. Some of the notes had personal touches, but most read something like this:

Dear Jane,

By now you've heard that I'm running for congress against John Boehner in Ohio's 8th District. In order to mount a strong, purposeful campaign, I need the financial support of friends and family to help make our work effective. Please consider donating $500 so that we can continue to grow our staff and get our message out through the media. We need funding "angels" right now to help us. Please return your check as soon as possible in the self-addressed, stamped envelope provided. Thanks for making a difference with your support.

Warmest Regards, Tom Poetter

I tried to write 10–20 cards per night. I addressed them, stamped them, and mailed them the next day. By the time I wrote the cards, I was absolutely exhausted from the day. I probably made a million mistakes, left words out, no doubt. I trashed a number of cards each night because of mistakes. A few times, I fell asleep at my chair. But I kept pushing. What I wanted to see is if I could make a dent in this barrier, the lack of support from close at hand. I felt like every politician faced this, but I had to break through if we were going to hire a staff member. And I resolved to do so. I thought deep down that people who got my handwritten plea might consider the time and effort it took to write to them, and that I did it myself. Subtext: I wasn't a huge star, didn't have a big staff, and needed support. I am handwriting these notes myself! Please send a check!

As Marv and I called potential donors on the phone each night, we decided that even people who responded lukewarmly would get a mailer. We had several layers of responses on our calls to potential donors: 1) Laughing, you and your campaign are a joke, "No" (no mailer sent); 2) Not interested in your campaign or politics, "No" (no mailer sent); 3) Glad you are running, think it's great, but "No" (send a mailer); 4) Wow, what a courageous fool you are, "I'll consider it" (send a mailer); 5) You are crazy for running, and just for that yes, "I'll contribute" (try to get a credit card commitment on the phone, or at least a numerical amount for pledge, and send a follow up mailer noting the amount in the note); 6) We need more people like you in politics, I like you a lot, "here's my credit card number" (Yes! Send a thank you note in the mail); 7) You have my vote, "can you send me a mailer so I can get a check mailed out to you?" (Yes! …).

Over the next few weeks, the needle moved, if ever the slightest little bit. I absolutely loved seeing fruits from our labor through the phones and the mail. Each day I picked up the mail at our P.O. Box, which provided a great thrill. Some days we received three or four responses, most with checks in them. And we started to see some progress. Some of the checks included handwritten notes of support. These became wonderful treasures, and adorned the walls of the office. I would sometimes look at them when things got bleak, which they often did. My goal from this push: I wanted to have two or three months of salary in the bank for our new finance director/campaign manager. That meant continuing to watch our spending and banking everything we made on the phone and through the mail. Marv and I pushed toward a total of $20,000 in the bank.

And so I heard back on the phone from Ben Shepherd and The Jackson Team that Clyde Tate had been considering the job. But time slipped away from us each day, agonizingly, especially with the Primary fast approaching on May 5. I didn't ask Ben if I could contact Clyde myself because I knew he would say, "No, I have it all under control," but I resolved to find Clyde Tate online and make my own personal pitch. I struck pay dirt through LinkedIn, finding him listed there, but struggled to figure out how to get a message directly to him. The site puts up all kinds of barriers to this type of activity if you don't know how to use it (which I don't, and I still don't get LinkedIn) and you aren't willing to pay for an upgrade. But I finally got a short message somehow to him—I can't even describe the steps since I simply got lucky bumping around—and he responded. We set up a phone call for that night. When I reached him on the phone, I asked a simple question after he interviewed me for a few minutes, "Are you willing to join us in Ohio? We need your focus, expertise, spirit."

After just a short moment, Clyde said, "No, I'm not coming, Tom. I want to do something different than running a campaign finance team, and if I did take a campaign job, I want to do more than finance. I want to manage a campaign. I realize that you are offering the opportunity to do both, but I feel like the focus the first few months with your campaign is to get the financial part of the campaign in order and running, then I might get some experience as overall manager. But at this point, I just don't want to get back into it."

"Fine," I said, "but if you change your mind in the next few days, give me a call."

I knew he wasn't going to call. It's the last time I ever spoke with Clyde Tate.

SOMETHING
HAS TO GIVE!

I have a close friend from childhood with whom I have consulted periodically throughout my entire life. Sometimes we talk about issues or events
that present a fun life twist, sometimes about serious matters. At one point
just after the New Year, he said to me, coaching me on running my campaign:

Stay out of the money.
Just run a good campaign on your own.
Don't worry about party apparatchiks or what anyone else says.
Learn and study and speak your mind.
You can't win anyway, so don't get bogged down with that.
Just be your self.

I didn't listen to him. I knew that his approach would be a dead end, just
like my approach would be. But I didn't want to run a meaningless, power-
less, helpless campaign with no money, no strategy, no expertise, no learning.
What good was that? How did that make a contribution? Periodically, when
things got tough and I needed to get back to basics, I thought of him and his
advice and how I ignored it. I would regret my decision periodically throughout the campaign, especially when the going got really tough.

But for now, I decided I had to right the ship. I took steps. I let Ben
Shepherd know that Clyde was out (he already knew, of course!) and then I
dug up my notes from my phone discussion with the county party chair when

we had discussed potential campaign staffers last month. I let Ben know that the person who stuck in my memory from our conversation was Katarina Vicar, a former finance director for a congressional campaign in New York who had come home to Butler County last year in order to address several health concerns. Desperate now, Ben said, "Give her a call, it can't hurt."

I discussed the matter with Marv. I said, "We have to do something. The big guys can't land a staffer and a local is going to have to do it. Let's follow up with Katarina and find out what she's got to offer."

"Go for it," Marv offered.

I called Katarina on the phone, got her by surprise, introduced myself, and she said, "It's taken long enough for you to call me."

I laughed, of course, but she didn't. I said, "Well, I'm calling you now. Tell me a little bit about your campaign experience."

I liked what I heard. She said that she had run campaigns in New York City and New York State after moving to Brooklyn from Ohio. She got sick, had to move home to Ohio, and had been recovering from cancer treatments and waiting for her next campaign opportunity. She had worked hard on the Obama Ohio campaign in 2012 and learned a lot. She said, "Running against Boehner has been a lifelong dream. This is the most important race in the country. I think I can help you."

I suggested that we meet at a fundraiser in Hamilton on Monday, March 10, at Jodie Grandview's home, a supporter who had offered early on to host a fundraising event. We had been working off and on over the past month with her on a guest list, and then got some help from another Hamilton friend in attempt to stir up interest and attendance at the event. Jodie, basically, had completely dropped the ball in terms of working up a guest list then cultivating it on the phone and on line. That's the only way to get anyone to come to anything. But no matter the attendance or lack thereof, it would be a good opportunity for Katarina to hear my short pitch and make a decision if she liked us enough to join the team. At this point, it had nothing to do with whom we liked or not. We needed help. And we had no time to lose.

Every single day in early March brimmed with work and activity. Marv and I continued to cultivate our list from Erik and I continued to write donor letters. My classes rolled toward Spring break, and I continued going to committee meetings, reading for classes, grading papers, writing, and meeting with students. I squeezed the campaign in around these central events, and spent the last part of Sam's senior hockey season traveling to matches, getting away from it all with Chris. That gave a particular pleasure, as Sam and his hockey team excelled.

Early in the month I had another one of several meetings with student leaders from the College Democrats. They and their friends pushed toward spring break with their studies and activities, trying to work volunteering on my campaign into the mix. I asked if there were any way that the group could work on the primary with us. They volunteered everyone, but the fact of the matter turned out to be the same story, no different than it was at the beginning: students couldn't get other students organized to help out, and we didn't have enough help to coach the students who did show up to work. We needed Katarina more than ever.

March 10, 2014

GRANDVIEW HOUSE PARTY

For weeks, with everything else spinning around, we had an offer for a house party fundraiser floating in space. Jodie Grandview liked our campaign and wanted to host a fundraiser in her home. I assigned Marv to it, but he had a hard time getting ahold of Ms. Grandview, and when we did finally make contact, we realized that she had done nothing to secure a group of people to attend and donate. So we asked Vince Allman, a local who had run for county offices, to contact a list of his people in Hamilton and Fairfield and to be a co-host of the party. He agreed at the last minute and worked hard to generate an audience. Seven people showed up. We had expected 30.

So it turned out to be a cozy, though disappointing party in terms of numbers. Katarina came in ahead of the scheduled time, and we had a few minutes to chat before I made a pitch. I remember on this occasion that one or two of the guests acted like skeptics, and they stick out when there are only seven people present: "Why did <u>you</u> get in the race? What would <u>you</u> do about local business development? Be specific." The questions had an edgy tone I heard sometimes on the campaign trail, and the person asking the business question, as it turned out, of course, had his own self-interest in lowering the tax burden on business start ups, like his! Overall, with citizens like these, I got this general impression from them, like, I didn't have a political pedigree, so what did I know about anything? I gave some answers, but I could tell I didn't satisfy them.

And, of course, almost everyone had a self-interest that they masked, then revealed it with the big ask, sometimes veiled, sometimes not, "What can your candidacy do for me?" The personal politics on the campaign trail had a purity to it, with people wanting me to succeed by fighting for big ideas against a big opponent, and an impurity to it, with people hoping merely to advance their own interests through the political process, either by securing a better political environment for their agenda or for their own personal, usually financial, gain. This is something I never really got used to on the campaign trail. I never really understood why party members acted so skeptical, perhaps even negative around me, whether they wanted a larger objective achieved or their own micro-objective. What made them take this mostly negative, self-serving approach as I worked to build a message and an identity on the campaign trail? Why didn't they just help me?

After my short talk and q/a, we drank soda and wine and ate from the snack spread that Ms. Grandview had prepared. Very nice. Katarina and I had a chance to talk privately for a few minutes, in between her attempts at sidling up to Vince, whom she adored and wanted to marry on first blush. She said, "You're the real deal, Poetter, I think this will work out. We can work on a few things to get you ready to take next steps. But you can do it. I wasn't sure before tonight. We need to get started."

I agreed, but after we parted that night, with just a small amount of money for the campaign raised, I called Ben Shepherd to let him know how well it had gone with Katarina. But Ben said, "You didn't offer her the job, did you?"

I said, "No, we didn't make anything official. She's coming to Oxford Wednesday to talk things over with us."

"Good," Ben said, "that gives Erik and me a chance to interview her tomorrow on the phone. This is big, Tom. It has to be the right person. You can't fix it if you have to fire the person in a month and start over again. She has to be in for the long haul."

"I know. I get it."

"Okay, we'll be in touch."

So I started waiting again for others to help me make decisions that I thought I could make. I realized that Erik and Ben were trying to protect me, but I felt so disempowered. Things had been moving quickly, and they continued to do so. We didn't have any time to waste!

March 12, 2014

You're Hired!

When we met with Katarina Wednesday, Marv and I didn't know anything in particular about her phone conversation with Erik and Ben, but we knew it had happened and had gotten word from them that we could proceed.

"Why didn't you tell me they were going to call?"

"Because they took it out of my hands, the final decision. They just let me know this morning in an email that they approve of you. High praise, if you ask me."

Her mood turned, "Yeah, I know, I really impressed them with my knowledge of finance, the people and money players in Ohio, the amount of money I raised in New York on my last campaign. They think I'm going to be great for you, Poetter."

She smiled, and I felt as though we would get along well. I wanted her to know how glad we were to have her on board. But in front of Marv, I wanted her to also know more deeply what I thought this was.

"Katarina, I want to do well, and I want to take this to the next level. But I'm not a slave to the campaign. I won't be here 24 hours a day. You might, but I'm not going to be. I have already stressed out my marriage in the first five months of this. And I'm not going to ruin a 27-year relationship with my wife.

98

And I'm not going to miss any of my son Sam's high school baseball games in March, April, and May. I'm not going to be the dad who all of a sudden disappears. And my first priority is my Miami work. There is no way I'll do anything to jeopardize the time I spend on classes, getting ready, working with students. That's sacred territory."

She reacted swiftly, "Anyone can put his heart and soul into something for eight months, Poetter. It's only eight months, then it's over. You have to get tougher. Tell people what you are going to do and make a commitment to it. You can't run a half-assed campaign. That's a crock. I don't want to get into something where the candidate is out of touch, not present, ineffective. Are you in this or not?"

I responded, "I am in this. Of course, I am. You don't know what I've been through. I've been in it up to my eyeballs for five months. We need your help and expertise, but I'm in charge of this campaign, and I set the schedule."

"Ha!" she laughed mockingly. "First order of business is that I set the schedule. I'm the campaign manager. You do what I tell you to do. If you don't, the whole thing breaks down. Do you understand?"

"That's not going to happen, not in a million years."

The test of wills, the Smash Up Derby of a campaign gets encapsulated in the relationship between the candidate and a campaign manager. Our journey toward a balance of wills, of talent, of effort, would last from this moment through the very last moment of the campaign. I'm not sure that we ever reached balance, equilibrium, but the energy we generated kept our inertia in tact.

I had heard this scenario before. It sounded a lot like Cindy Winter's blanket statement so many months before at the kitchen table in my home. Somewhere in the folklore of campaigns rested this agreed upon mantra—about the hierarchy, about the system, how it's supposed to work in terms of control and power—that the campaign manager tells people, even the candidate, what to do and they do it. I had lost so much of myself already, I just couldn't imagine giving up all control to someone who hadn't been at headquarters yet for 15 minutes. SO, at the same time that I hired Katarina Vicar to be my campaign manager, I started fighting with her, on almost every front. This created a sort of equilibrium. I wouldn't be bullied into doing anything I didn't want to do (that didn't actually work) and I would have some autonomy, some say, some control of how things would go moving forward (not so much!).

Marv and I spent a few hours auditioning on the phone with Katarina, making donor calls and mostly coming up empty. She critiqued us, gave us good pointers, and pushed me to close, to make the hard ask (a specific request to fund the campaign immediately at a certain dollar amount). I resisted, said it wasn't in my nature, that I hated call time, and didn't want to be there. This is the worst, hardest part of the campaign.

"But it's the part I love the most, Poetter. That's why I'm here. I love call time."

Settling into Life with a New Boss

Over the next several days, we hired Katarina officially as our finance director/campaign manager, worked to get her employment profile set up with the state party so she would be paid, and we settled into a mini-, short-term routine with Katarina. Marv ran call time, while Katarina listened and coached us. We used the list we had been using from Erik, and it yielded some small donations. The list had issues, but it was the best thing we had or could get our hands on at this point. Katarina knew that, but said, "Boys, we are going to work this list, and the friends and family list until they are bled dry. By that time, I'll have new lists for us to call. And we are going to call donors in other states, like New York, and California, where people actually support congressional campaigns for Democrats all over the country. We will put together lists from races where underdogs put up a fight against established candidates. Those are our people! Poetter, you are going to call hundreds of supporters in New York, and they are going to give you the business and give you money. We have to get you ready!"

I found this next step of calling New Yorkers to be ominous mentally, and we argued over my weekly commitment to call time. I said I would go no higher than 21 hours a week on call time. That's three hours a day, or about 700 calls per week. Over the 32 weeks with Katarina, that would be over 20,000 calls. That's all I could imagine doing with the rest of my work schedule and other campaign events. Katarina argued that calls meant money. If I dialed, the calls would yield, and as I called more and got better at it, we would earn more and more.

"Poetter, you have to do more call time. We can't get there without your commitment. No one else can do it. We could raise money through PACs and unions, but we have to do that <u>and</u> call time, not one or the other. There is no way around this. You can do it. I'll be with you every step of the way. But we have to get to 30 hours."

"I won't do it. I'm going to hand you my schedule for call time every week, and that's all I'm going to do. I don't care what you say, or what you do. That's all I'm doing. You build your schedule around me. I can barely make it through the three hours each day. It's grueling, it's inhumane, it's awful, it's demoralizing. If I'm going to make 20,000 calls, I have to do it over time. That gives you time to get me some great numbers together on our new lists anyway. I think it will work out fine. It is what it is."

"It's not good enough, Poetter. All the statewide candidates are calling at least six hours a day. That's what it takes. They are making millions of dollars. Their races are different, but they are more committed than you are."

"They are career politicians, all of them in the state house as representatives or are lifelong politicians with connected families. This is what they do. Their jobs allow for it, so do their families, so do their dispositions. This isn't my job. I can only do what I can do. While we have been arguing, I've been sketching my call time for next week."

I handed her my call schedule, based on the hours that I had available in my own work and family schedule. Exactly 21 hours. Most of the call time hours came during the day. I smiled, and she fumed, storming out of the office, infuriated. As always, I knew she would come back, with a better attitude, and get right back to work. I have to say, in all my years, I have never, ever had a relationship with a person whom I could upset and not worry about it. Over time in other relationships, I have danced around hard issues, always held back, never spoke my mind in fear of losing the person, maybe saying the wrong thing. For whatever reason, and I'll probably never be able to pinpoint why, I never worried about this with Katarina.

The truth of the matter was that I knew she was the right choice for this job. She's talented and committed and worked hard and believed in me, and desperately wanted to run hard against Boehner. But I had to fight for my life with her at nearly every turn. Sometimes things hummed along nicely, and then a situation would arise where I had to take a stand, and I always did. I never held back, and it always caused an explosion on her part, or my part. Near the end, if things got bad, I reached a point where I didn't care if Katarina walked away. We had accomplished all that we could by a certain point. We couldn't gain any more ground, and I think she knew that and felt the end to be near. That caused some tension, but she never quit and I never fired her. I'm glad for that.

During this time period I probably got a little more irritable because I had to go on a crash diet with Chris. I couldn't get into any of my dress clothes comfortably, and with the Legacy Dinner in Columbus coming up, I had to look decent. At that statewide meeting, we would be meeting elected officials, potential donors, and get endorsed for our race by the state party, despite our primary challenger. That meant I had to drop at least 10 pounds in two weeks. I told Chris, and we immediately took on the Dr. Oz cleanse diet, which consisted of hot lemon water in the morning, a shake for breakfast, salad for lunch, and a piece of chicken or fish and some rice plus salad again in the evening. We had some nuts for snacks, and drank lots of water. I lost 10 pounds by March 15, in a two-week period. We started the diet on February 28. I got my collar buttoned and my tie tied in mid March. A miracle, really. It proved to be the case that I kept the weight off until the very end of the campaign. I liked being able to get into my clothes, plus I felt nervous enough most days, and got so busy that I ate a lot less. Losing weight is one benefit of running for an unwinnable seat in congress.

March 15, 2014

Ohio Democratic Party Legacy Dinner, Columbus, Ohio

Just about everything that could go wrong went wrong at the Legacy Dinner. We got there on time, and Chris went along so she could see an old high school and college friend who had a place in the upper level of the state's party, having served in Ohio Governor Strickland's cabinet 2006–2010. That's about the extent of the positives, except for the fact that my pants fit and I had a decent meal for the first time in two weeks. Katarina got there on her own, since Chris and I left from Oxford and didn't pick her up.

When we got to the event, Katarina and I arrived around the same time and took seats next to each other in one of the ballrooms for the endorsement meeting. At the meeting, Chris Redfern, the state party chair, greeted us warmly and thanked us for being there. But he didn't invite me to say anything to the assembled members. He rambled on, welcoming people at the beginning, setting up an air of control and power from the podium, introducing people, asking them to weigh in and say a word or two.

All of the statewide candidates came to the meeting, and each gave a short speech similar to the one they would give at the dinner in a few hours and also similar to the ones I had been hearing them give on the stump at events all around Ohio. Once again, they proved to be remarkably confident, poised, knowledgeable, energetic, eminently electable, all of them. I couldn't imagine the Republicans putting up candidates that could come close to them in terms of experience and competence: David Pepper for Attorney General; Nina Turner for Secretary of State; John Patrick Carney for State Auditor;

and Connie Pillich for State Treasurer. Each of them gave rousing, shortened versions of their stump speeches, well-oiled, seasoned pros, all of them. As I watched them speak I wondered, "How in the world can I get to that point? They are so good, with well-honed, moving stories and insights about their own lives and politics." The fact was that I couldn't get there with so little experience. I needed more time in front of people, more crucible moments that would lead me to narrow, define, and clarify my story. These painful and joyful opportunities would come soon enough. But for now, I just listened.

When it came time for the endorsement part of the meeting, Mr. Refern read the names of people and their races and asked for a motion and a second from the floor to endorse. Certainly this was a missed opportunity to speak to this gathering; but I really wasn't ready anyway to speak to this seasoned crowd. No discussion followed the listing. The group passed the slate and the meeting adjourned. The next part of the evening would be the most important. I received access with a VIP pass, thanks to county chair Nicole, and she met me and took me around to the various rooms set aside for candidates and donors. I was introduced as "the guy running against Boehner." I said, "Yep, that's me. Nice to meet you."

I didn't make the mistake of admitting I didn't know people. I just tried to chat it up. I met several people that I knew about from the news and enjoyed talking with them, including PG Sittenfeld from Cincinnati City Council, who would go on in the coming year to challenge former governor Stickland for the U.S. Senate nomination on the Democratic side in the race against Rob Portman. He was kind, very approachable, interesting. But I stood around some just watching the crowd and trying to fit in, and ran into some awkward conversations. Some donors cared very little about my race. Of course, they thought I had no chance no matter how competent I seemed. They were right. They kept their money. Others, though, were generous, themselves somewhat disengaged with the whole big-time political scene all wrapped in the evening, glad to have some hearty, honest conversations about politics and the process.

All the while I followed Nicole around the hall meeting people, Katarina was shut out. She didn't get a VIP pass. So she stewed and acted upset when we ran into her before dinner as we made our way to our seats. The kick in the pants came when we saw where we had been seated. The county table landed as far away from the podium and stage and head table as was possible in the gigantic hall. Several thousand people packed the place, listening to political speeches, sometimes turning the speaker off and just having their own conversations at the table while they ate or basically partied. Wow, did I hate this part of the night. I felt so weird just talking during the speeches. Later, this would become a marker for me about the audience and how serious they were about the work at hand. Talking during the speech = rude.

And Nicole herself just stewed, and almost brimmed over with anger with the table placement. I think she was mostly embarrassed. I guess at the time I figured, "What do you expect for a county party that has exactly zero elected public officials except for one city Mayor?" But it hurt her, and she had delivered a viable candidate to run against Boehner, me! That meant absolutely nothing, really.

One silver lining beyond the meal being decent and Chris having a good time with her old friend at dinner, came when our candidate for governor, Ed Fitzgerald, gave his rousing, wonderful talk. It would be his high water mark, however, falling prey later in the campaign when Governor Kasich's henchman released word that Ed had not had a valid driver's license for years. He fell from contention to out of contention in a few days, ruining the state party chair's career and sealing the doom of every talented statewide candidate in the room. Without a viable governor candidate, there typically remains little hope of winning the other statewide offices.

At the end of the night, we got to spend a few minutes with Erik, who graciously walked around with us talking about next steps. For all intents and purposes, he had done what he could do for us to this point and would not play any significant role in the campaign after tonight. But the rush out of the place turned mad, like a cattle stampede. We barely made it out alive. It was invigorating, exciting, maddening all at once, and I vowed to myself that no matter what happened to me in this race that I would never participate in an event like this one for as long as I lived. I really didn't like establishment politics, the feel of the place, the power, the cliques, the seeming impossibility of having any impact on it as an outsider. There's no way I could ever become an insider.

Clark County Democrats' Spring Chili Cook Off

The Clark County Democratic Women invited me to their chili cook off way back in October. I asked the county party members assembled then point blank if they would host a fundraiser like they did for the gubernatorial candidate Ed Fitzgerald, but they said I could ask for money and give a speech at the Winter Chili Cook-Off hosted by the Clark County Democratic Women just as well, killing two birds. It sounded like a great invitation at the time. The only problem with this equation? I could ask for money, but the event would not be a fundraiser for me, and I would walk away without a dime. People have to bring their checkbooks to a fundraising event with the expressed intent of making a contribution, or nothing (or very little) will happen. Not a great formula for any kind of success, really, only bitterness.

The event had gotten snowed out in February. I had been in the car as the snow came down in blankets and got the cancel call just before starting the wintery trek to Springfield. I am so grateful I didn't drive all the way there; the weather that day in February turned horrendous, and deadly for motorists. On this later March day, the weather was great, and I sped off with Katarina in tow. She wanted me to make calls all the way there while she drove, after we had already spent three hours on the phone. No way that would happen. She wasn't driving, and I wasn't calling! I just didn't have the stamina nor did I trust her to drive me anywhere. That wouldn't change for eight months.

When we got to the event, we brought a new energy. Katarina really excelled at meeting people, engaging them, making friends. She also quickly made enemies, suffering no fools, jumping to assumptions about people and situations. Sometimes she read signs and words and notions and ideas dead on; sometimes she missed the boat. At any rate, that's what she would do, time and again. Most of the time she hit the mark and impressed. Tonight we made new friends, talked with everyone, and began, basically, a new campaign.

Of course, tradition rules at events like this one, and the women had a long history of hosting this event and taking their chili seriously. I got invited to be a judge, and spent time with the panel, one member whom we had met before who touted her past experiences on a national level with energy policy. I never could quite pin down what her position had been. Maybe she didn't ever really do anything. We'll never know. But we didn't believe a word she said, thought she no doubt had been stretching the truth, but it didn't matter because I turned out to be no match for her. I had no idea what she was ever talking about, so I just listened and nodded my head. That's the only strategy that worked with her, and I had to repeat it on the campaign trail with her several times over the next several months.

So I had to taste all of the chili soups, about 10 of them, as a judge. I have to admit, my taster got tired after about two soups, and I didn't think I did a very good job of it. I like chili as a general rule, but liked only two of the ones people brought and hated eight of them! I guess all my life I had been spoiled by Campbell's soup, my mom's chili, and my wife's outstanding homemade chili. We host a Super Bowl party at our house for friends every winter, and Chris' chili always rocks, beef or chicken based. None of the chili soups at the event even came close to my lifetime top three, including Campbell's. I went along with the other two judges, both Clark County Women, and the new winner got anointed.

When I gave my stump talk after people had eaten their sampling of chili and other foods carried in, it generated no interest. I got very little give back from the crowd in terms of eye contact, clapping, interest. It's hard to tell what they thought, or wanted. The rest of the candidates there for county and state rep races had very little to offer in their short speeches. None of them had much of a message or a campaign direction. And almost all of them had very little political experience, most even less than me. Later, one of them came up to me and said, "I just hate following you as a speaker, you're so good."

I felt shocked by that, and very appreciative at the same time. I knew I could give a talk, I did it all the time at school and in life in so many other venues. Maybe people just expected since I was a professor that I already knew I was good and didn't need any positive feedback. But I needed something from the audience, especially while using this new language and doing different things with talks and speeches and ideas.

SPRING
BREAK WEEK

All this week while we celebrated Spring Break at school the team (Katarina, Marv, and I) really hunkered down on call time and made some progress. We began to come to a point where we had exhausted what we could do with the existing names and numbers we had for donors. Katarina had been working on several new lists, and we geared up to start them. She wanted me to do several things on my phone calls: 1) hit the donor with a hard ask early in the call; 2) ask for a specific amount, the number Katarina put on the call sheet; and 3) to NOT stay on the phone chatting or talking politics—wasted time chatting meant making fewer calls ... fewer calls meant less money.

Well, needless to say, I had a really hard time with all three of these. My classic mistake call went something like this: Dial, answer, donor picks up...

"Hi, Marcia, this is Tom Poetter calling from Oxford, I'm running as the Democrat against John Boehner in District 8. How are you today?"

Many people just hung up on me, even after answering. Hard knocks, especially if we thought the person could make a sizeable donation. Katarina hated this and always blamed me for hang-ups. Obviously not my fault, but obviously my fault. If the donor wanted to talk, she often laughed (running against Boehner is ludicrous, but somehow interesting in a macabre sort of way to people interested in politics and prone to supporting candidates with money), then asked how I got in the race, how I was doing, did we have a chance? I usually engaged the person, following his or her direction on topic, and simply talked with them. I enjoyed this part of the game.

Sometimes after a few minutes of really connecting with the person I felt awkward asking specifically for a donation. Sometimes the donor let me off the hook: "Well, I suppose you have a lot of calls to make, and you are probably going to ask me for money. I can give you $100 today." The donor-offered number typically came in below the hard ask number Katarina had scripted on the call sheet. A classic mistake. Make the hard ask FIRST and make the donor say no, and offer a lower total but higher than what they might suggest themselves on first blush. Or retell the story and basically re-pitch, or beg with Katarina's lines: "This is the race. Now is the time. We can do something about gridlock in Washington. Don't send an incompetent incumbent back to congress again, for the 13th time!"

Sometimes I really connected on the phone with a potential donor and he just said no to my ask. One donor we thought we had hook, line, and sinker, said no, and I sounded so disappointed that he sent a "guilt" check just a week later. He wrote in a note with the check: "You sounded so hurt when I said no that it haunted me. Hope this helps." It did. He wrote the check for $250, which he agreed later to repeat two more times before the general election. What a doll.

I flat out just lost some people on the phone. I said the wrong thing and offended. I let the person off the hook for whatever reason, and then the person never responded to later calls or letters. Many people just said they were tired of politics, seeing their money go to waste, donating to candidates who lost, who had no chance, who disappointed them. I assured them that while I most assuredly would lose, their support meant a robust, vocal campaign against the sitting Speaker of the House of Representatives who faced no Democratic opposition on the ballot in 2012, not even a straw candidate.

Ideally the person would say yes to the hard ask, but then you could haggle with her good naturedly if she thought the ask number too high. Sometimes a donor offered more than I asked for. I got better at the hard ask:

" … Thanks for taking my call, Simon. We really need your help. Can you donate $500 to our campaign today?"

Say nothing until the potential donor speaks. Silence, so hard to do. I got better at it, but I messed up calls, too. And if I couldn't get a commitment, I pounced when the donor waivered with more reasons showing clear need and how much he/she could help.

The best calls involved connecting with the donor, making a hard ask, having the person say yes, and then taking a credit card number. Easy, the money went directly from the call to our account. These calls over the course of the campaign were few and far between. I'd say maybe 100 out of 20,000 calls turned out this way. If the person wanted to receive a mailer, I put his or her name on my short list and sent the mailer out that day or the next day first thing. Many donors were great about acting on the commitment. Sometimes they even sent more than I asked for. Rarely they sent less than they agreed to. Over time, these calls became more and mc re enjoyable. The mindless dialing—the hang-ups, the nasty harangues from potential donors who had an ax to grind with the system (usually not me, but still), the routine, the failure—took its toll.

I hated call time.

Katarina loved call time. She lived for it. She prepared for it. She got paid for it!

Besides call time, we worked on my speech outline and format, hoping to improve people's reaction to me at events. We found out that I absolutely lost the crowd when I talked about education and women's rights and immigration and voter rights and healthcare. Almost anything substantive and of interest to me fell flat in the room. Even solid Democrats who cared about these issues wanted next to nothing to do with these topics. They wanted me to bash Boehner, easy to do. They wanted to hear about jobs, support for public programs, jobs. Did I say jobs? Easy to do, but not in my wheelhouse. I used Paul Krugman as a guide on the economy. His work helped me create arguments for continuing public support for programs and for having a government contributing a strong financial stake in the economy, essential for overall fiscal health. Some of this fell on deaf ears as well.

And I continued to work on connecting with the College Democrats. Two very strong student leaders wanted to help. But, both in their senior year spring semesters, they just couldn't muster any real time commitment or any critical mass of people together to help us. We had two consecutive Tuesday evenings where a few students came to headquarters and made canvassing phone calls for the primary coming up. That was great, but the students didn't stick, didn't return. They got tired, went on spring break, and headed toward graduation. They didn't have time for our campaign. That changed later when seven Miami students became our blessed interns in the Fall. But that development was a long way off.

CAMPAIGN JUGGERNAUT

When I look back on the entire campaign from start to finish, I remember this two-week period in early April as wonderful—grueling, but wonderful. My classes and work hummed along as the semester wound down. We had been getting more publicity surrounding the campaign with the primary approaching, and this created a buzz, some excitement, all around me. I enjoyed that to some degree. I couldn't escape it now even if I tried. The only way to escape would be to lose the primary. And Sammy started playing his last season of high school baseball. The weather cooperated and I took leave each night he played to enjoy watching his games with Chris, and Mitch often accompanied us. And Sam and Chris both had April birthdays, so we celebrated and spent quality time together in the evenings. The calm before the storm, as they say.

The calm yielded a very serious question, as the topic of the primary started coming up and it generated some concern, and for Katarina, a considerable amount of panic: What were we actually doing to assure that we would win the primary against Guyette on May 6? Well, I didn't think I could lose to Matt Guyette under any circumstances, no matter what I did or didn't do. I was just a better candidate. But we received warnings from several county chairs that we had to make more voter contacts to assure we got the votes we needed. Sometimes weird things can happen when unknown candidates face off in a primary. Maybe the outcome depends on whose name appears first on the ballot. Maybe one candidate is perceived to be incompetent for some reason. Maybe one candidate succeeds in smearing the other at the last minute and it sticks. Who knows? But plenty of people who should have won primaries have lost them, even decisively. We decided not to lose.

That meant that while Katarina worked herself to the bone, continued to battle her cancer, worked out each day, and ate like a bird, she did both the big lift of getting the financial aspect of the campaign in gear while simultaneously getting a team together to focus on voter contact, all very difficult, a 22-hour a day job, with little infrastructure and few volunteers. So she started from scratch. And she planned. She planned to start canvassing, which I had only done sparingly in the past when I worked on a local school levy campaign. But I had never gone door-to-door on my own campaign. She planned that we would start phone banking in our headquarters, as many nights a week as possible, with a short script encouraging Democratic primary voters to show up at the polls to get me on the November ballot. The only way to do that was to show up and vote for me May 6. I had been keeping track of names and addresses and phone numbers and email addresses of people who had come to past events and gave their names as potential volunteers. Katarina mined this list, and started putting people in place to work. On some nights in April and early May, headquarters buzzed, with an energy straight out of a TV or movie script. While she managed the campaign, she did donor research, refining lists and pushing me each day with new numbers, new people, new frontiers of fundraising. It's no secret: the more you call, the more you make. And with the right donor phone numbers, paydirt.

We actually started making money for the campaign. And we needed it. We knew that we wanted to have some kind of media campaign in the summer and fall. That cost money. We knew that we needed more paid staffers. That cost money. We knew we needed more campaign materials, although Katarina was loathe to waste any money on yard signs and buttons, what she and future staffers would call "chum," derogatorily, after bait dumped into an open area to attract fish. The staff would tell horror stories for months about all the people they met who cared little about what campaigns really are (efforts to get people out to vote for your candidate) and just wanted the chum, yard signs and pins and such. Katarina would say, "No one ever won a campaign because they had more yard signs. Yard signs don't target voters, they are random, and have no impact." I argued they had a psychic impact internally on campaign workers and others who liked to see some fruit of their labor, like a sign they can put in their yard or a button to wear on their coat or shirt. We went round and round about it, and I finally just went behind

Katarina's back and placed an order for chum later, a one-time deal after the primary. That material made it all the way through the end of the campaign; we never could use it all. But people loved the buttons and putting a sign in their yard. It silenced our critics, but created tension inside the campaign.

While this was going on all at once, I kept preparing for big events coming up. Most of the counties had spring events before the primary, especially Miami County (April 14) and Mercer County (April 24) and they had invited me to appear. Darke County had a summer picnic after the primary, and Butler County had a Spring Fling the week after the primary once the slates got set. Clark County already had its chili cook off. And Preble County had its Women's Group Spring Event April 13. Tomorrow.

April 13, 2014
PREBLE COUNTY DEMOCRATIC WOMEN

Truth be told, there are very few Democrats in Preble County. It might be the reddest county in Ohio, if not the U.S.A. Just after I declared my candidacy for the seat and right before the 2013 elections on a trip up to St. Marys to visit family, Obama protesters—dressed in Obama masks with Hitler mustaches—commandeered the main intersection in Eaton. Their beef, emblazoned across their signs and placards? Obamacare is proof that Obama is a Nazi. Wow. Stunning. Chris, said, "These are your people, honey," completely mocking the impossible situation of running for a seat where there are literally ½ the needed votes necessary to win—statistically, no matter how you slice it given past elections and the registered voting public in this region. Having the president attend a campaign dinner or rally would do no Democrat any good in this region. I would definitely welcome that kind of interaction, but it would cost me votes. Truth.

I still haven't really gotten over the Obama Hitler images, and we still laugh about how extreme the politics and the people are in Preble County. But for several months, a woman who lives in Eaton and works in Oxford had been talking with me about having an event during which her group could meet me in Eaton. I gladly accepted her invitation, once again hoping for 50 people to show up and give us $50 each. Instead, we got 20 people in a community room in Eaton, not really a bad turnout and a tribute to the work that the Democratic women had been doing in the county over several decades. Only a few people at the event made a monetary contribution. We took home less than $300. It turned out later that this critical contact with the Preble County Democratic Women would lead us to our most productive relationship with a union in the area, a union that several of her friends' husbands and friends belonged to that would wind up supporting us with money and time on task helping us to the finish line.

Katarina and I had been so busy with call time and voter contact efforts that we spent no time preparing for the event. I basically had notes now that I prepared and took to events but never used. They never came out of my coat pocket. I had a few tried and true short bits that I used in talks. One bit that I had used since January was the one about Mom and Publisher's Clearinghouse. But that had tired and I rarely used it as an opener now. I usually started with a thank you to the crowd for supporting my campaign, a fiery litany of actions or inactions Boehner had committed against the nation or local citizens, pinpointing his lack of leadership and care for regular people. No matter how much Boehner talked about being a "little guy with a big job," he still operated like and embodied the life of a fat cat politician with a war chest and personal profiteering at the core of his life and work. And I hit several issues that had to do with our lives in this region that the speaker hardly ever addressed, jobs, wages, voting rights, women's rights, education, etc.

I did as good a job on this talk as I did on any one before it, some of them having been warmly received and exciting, others having fallen flat. I never got the impression that it was me; I always felt ready and that I did a good job of delivering. I began to believe that I could never, ever control the audience, or particularly the mood that any one negative person in the audience created with a comment or question. I wondered how performers felt with such wildly disparate audiences night after night, like a comedian trying to find her mojo when Detroit and Albuquerque are just flat out so different that the same shtick is bound to be taken ever so differently given the geography, the culture, the social climate, the weather!

On the way home, Katarina and I discussed tomorrow's event in Miami County, where I would be an after dinner speaker at the county party's annual Spring Fling. I would speak just ahead of state rep and statewide candidate for Auditor, John Patrick Carney of Columbus. I felt at ease about this test, one of several coming up, including the Mercer County Democratic Party Ox Roast (the name is from a bygone era—they don't roast an ox anymore, but they used to!) on April 24. These events felt big to me, like larger coming out parties. I wanted to do well, and I hoped that the events would lead to broader support, more volunteers, and more campaign contributions.

What I began to realize is that every single event and action and contact and hand shake and phone call and conversation with constituents mattered. I think I knew this, but I hadn't really gotten it straight in my head how much failure there would be in conjunction with successes. Politics is mostly about failure. You can never really appeal to everyone all the time. People are fallible. I'm not particularly good looking, or funny, or overly smart or impressive. Perhaps like Boehner says he is, I'm just a regular guy. But hardly anyone ever presented him or herself as just glad I was running. Everyone was a critic, or wanted something in particular. I learned this on the stump; I didn't know it before.

And I didn't know how small and insignificant these BIG events actually are in the grand scheme of things. They have to be done, but the participants are talking to people who are already going to vote for them. And the events do not get covered by media and have very little wider impact. But we took them so seriously, and paid a price for that. They tested us, and made us better. Tomorrow took its toll, long term.

FOREVER AND HENCEFORTH, THE CARNEY MASSACRE

I really didn't think that much about the Miami County Democratic Party's Spring Fling Dinner, what was at stake. I had been invited to speak, after having been endorsed at a party meeting in January, and I didn't really mind playing second fiddle to John Patrick Carney, State Representative and statewide candidate for auditor. I thought I could capitalize on the goodwill people had been showing me and the comfort I had been gaining doing my 6–8 minutes talks without notes. I figured that after dinner people wouldn't really want a long speech, and I wasn't the keynote speaker anyway. That duty and responsibility fell to Carney.

I refused, of course, to make calls on the 75 minute drive, but Katarina convinced me to make a few—once again the last time, I vowed, to ever do this on a car ride—and we actually got a few donors to give on the way up. In a moment of weakness, which turned out to be a blessing, I let Marv drive. The entire campaign team made the trek up together, Marv, Katarina, and me, the three amigos, at least for a while yet. Time went by quickly on the trip. I probably made 20 calls during the car ride, a first.

When we arrived, I distinctly remember John Patrick Carney and his aide, driving him, pulling into the parking lot at exactly the same time. I would describe Carney as having boyish good looks, with brown hair and an average build, slim, almost 6' tall, in his late 30s, young. He rolled out of his non-descript sedan with his jacket whirling through the air, throwing it on over his shoulders as he strolled in with his driver and finance manager, a really young man, in his 20s, dressed in a suit. We said hi on the way in, and they both responded very cordially to us.

I remember the assistant saying to me, "How did your call time go today? We did six hours. Great day. Made a boatload of money." He didn't even let me answer his question, and didn't care what we had done anyway. All he cared about was letting us know how committed to fundraising Mr. Carney was, and how well he was doing on the phone, making money hand over fist in an attempt to upend the vulnerable, incumbent, Republican Auditor Yost. I found this to be a common denominator among the young campaign hands we met over the months—they focused on measurable outcomes and figured out ways to tell you about them and to take credit for them. That's how you climb the campaign ladder—get a job, get results, push your story down every person's throat that you meet on the campaign trail, get noticed, get the next job.

I should have known I would be in for an ass-kicking that night after dinner when the county chair introduced the first speaker, a local, retired, popular politician who would entertain us with his rendition of the poem "Casey at the Bat," spoken in an Irish dialect. I knew the poem well so I followed him easily. Katarina said later that she couldn't understand a word he said and didn't get it. And she claimed to be a baseball fan! But the crowd absolutely ate it up. He acted out the parts, and really had the crowd in his palm. He got a rousing round of applause. He bowed like a Broadway thespian, and soaked it up.

The chair introduced me next, and I got a nice welcome from the crowd, though the staff had started clearing the tables, as the guests dug back into their desserts after being riveted by Casey's poem of plight. I made another lame, self-deprecating statement about how hard it was to follow "Casey at the Bat," then dug in with my story. Once again, I thought I nailed it, at first. At the same time, I knew that my stories had taken a little too long to develop, and I told one too many before getting into the meat of the matter on several issues, boring the crowd a little, I thought. I felt okay when I sat down; no standing ovation, and no one rushed the table to hand me a check or to get my autograph. But, fine.

Then the chair introduced John Patrick Carney.

When Mr. Carney took the podium, he commanded it and the crowd. He brought great energy to his speech, hitting the big, main themes he had talked about several times in other events I had seen him work. But this speech kept getting better, and better, with the crowd really resonating with his key points and applause lines. He didn't have a note. He just spoke to the crowd, from the heart. He told about being raised in a loving family, the 11th of 12 children. About being a devout Catholic. About sacrificing for family, and feeling the love of sacrifice from parents and siblings. About putting himself through college. About marrying his high school sweetheart. About the love of family, and the importance of education, especially about the responsibility for guaranteeing a good public education for every single child in Ohio. About knowing what it was like to work hard at any job necessary to make it through law school. About how hard he worked in politics to meet citizens, knocking on more doors than anyone ever had to win a house race against all odds. About things he accomplished in the state house for the poor, and the under-represented. About how decrepit and ineffectual the current administration in Columbus acted. About how he could bring stability and experience and knowledge and success to statewide office on our behalf. And on and on, never missing a beat, hitting every punch line, every detail of his story and speech without fail for 20 minutes, in perfect order and with perfect energy and timing.

Masterful.

When he finished, sweating now and with his coat off, the crowd rose to its feet as one with a tremendous roar of applause in approval. A standing ovation. I jumped to my feet, all the while feeling sorry for myself, overcome by the virtuoso performance of a young, brilliant, outstanding politician. Maybe people in the audience felt like Burt did when he first heard John Gilligan speak in the 1960s. Maybe Carney would become governor, or Senator, or President. As I clapped, however, my little world closed in on me.

This certainly wasn't a competition, but I felt really, really small, and defeated nonetheless. I knew at this moment, finally, that I was operating completely out of my league. I could not go to meetings like this one, be asked to give a talk, then look small, diminutive, especially when the other speakers rose to the occasion and nailed it. Yes, they had more experience. Yes, they had more on the ball and knew what to say and had been practicing for years. Yes, I really had no way of making up this lost ground in such a short time. But I had too many dates coming up and I couldn't be embarrassed again. This had to stop now!

The time between the end of Carney's speech and the end of the meeting and the after party time came as a blur. What I remember most about the time between the speeches and rolling myself into a fetal position in the back of the van was the rush of Democrats to Carney's side when the meeting adjourned to shake his hand and ask him a question and touch his sleeve. Absolutely no one came up to me. I might as well have been invisible. Carney absolutely owned the night, made a great splash. Kicked my ass, royally.

Never again, I pledged at that moment.

Thank goodness Marv had driven us up. He knew the way home. I was in no condition to drive.

I rode all the way home in a fetal ball in the backseat, not saying a word to Marv or Katarina except to scream out loud to the universe, about every 10-mile marker:

"John Patrick Carney kicked my ass! That's never, ever going to happen again! Dammit that's guy's a genius!!!"

Over and over and over every 10 miles. Marv and Katarina just let me grieve.

April 15, 2014
Aftermath—
Hard Work

We started early on Tuesday. I wanted to get right back at it after the debacle. First on the agenda, with Katarina: Explore the entire campaign to date for ways to beef up my public speaking, my speech, my ideas, the issues of concern, my stories. This is really right up my alley, and I had done some of this work so far, mostly on my own, but it wasn't good enough. Carney taught me that. I needed professional help.

To her credit, Katarina treated me with kid gloves.

"Look, it wasn't that bad. Really, Carney just hit it out of the park. He's really good looking, by the way."

"Stop it with the baseball allusions, Casey. I know he killed it, and me. I just can't stand losing."

"It's not a competition, we're all on the same side."

"The hell we are. We are on my side, and I can't look bad like that again. You saw it, a blood bath. Shit."

"You have really upped the swearing ante, I like it. We need more fire from you."

"Well, there's more where that came from if we don't get this right."

We worked several hours and hammered out some themes, very honestly collating the things that had been working the past month and the things that hadn't, coming up with some new ideas and issues and stories to foreground. We started putting together the rudiments of a speech that would hit listeners, show my depth and gravitas, and position me as electable,

123

at least to Democrats. How could I hope for any votes in this election if I couldn't even get the local Democrats to see me? And I started trying to memorize parts of it so I could say it all naturally, like the sections of the statewide candidates' speeches that they had committed to memory and delivered flawlessly. I wasn't going to the Mercer County Pig Roast on April 24 to get embarrassed by Connie Pillich, who would be the keynote speaker, running for the state treasurer position. I had heard her speak eloquently on the stump as well, a terrific speaker and state representative with her own wonderful story of serving in the military, and winning an unwinnable seat in the state house, just like Carney had.

We definitely had our work cut out for us.

In retrospect, of course, I can see again how seriously and how ludicrously I positioned these events. In some ways, I had it all right, and in some ways, all wrong. I had it right that the speakers at these events, the ones asked to keynote ahead of me because they were running for statewide office and had already served in political positions, brought it every time and worked hard at these events all over the state, every day, for every single dollar and every single vote they could muster. I had it wrong that it was personal, that I somehow was losing at these events. And I was wrong that they mattered that much, since so few people, so few voters, even just a small percentage of the Democrats I wanted to influence, actually came to the events, actually heard me. But the events happened, and they mattered to me, and I had to do better or I couldn't live with myself. I wanted to compete, and be fully in the race. I had to bring it, too, then! So we worked, and put a new stump speech together, and I practiced ...

April 19, 2014

LEARNING TO
WALK, WALKING
TO LEARN

With the primary election fast approaching, we knew we had to hit the streets and knock on as many Democratic doors as we could in Butler County before May 6. So Katarina put me with a local candidate, Suzi Rubin, running for the statehouse seat in District 53. A veteran on the local campaign trail, she had served on Monroe City Council for several years, and she turned out to be a great campaign teacher. We decided to do an introductory walk in Oxford, and over the next couple of weeks we branched out to Middletown (her hometown area) and Hamilton. She taught me the ropes, what to do, what to say, how to make the most of meetings with citizens at the door. Also, the campaign had excellent walking sheets with addresses and information on voters for every door to be knocked on. Suzi worked her routes with hand held maps and technology that entered data directly to the state party's vote builder database. I never graduated to that level, instead keeping track on paper of each interaction with staff then entering that data into the computer back at the office after the walks.

At first we walked together, Suzi and me. She followed my lead, allowing me to get as much experience, with coaching, as possible in such a short amount of time. I would say hello and introduce myself, and introduce Suzi. Lots of people in Oxford knew me, but even more knew Suzi from past campaigns. When we walked together in Oxford, we had a great time, meeting new friends and old friends, encouraging people to vote, talking about issues. Truly, as I found out on the campaign trail for months to come, knocking on doors turned out to be the most exhilarating and wonderful part of the campaign.

I had experience communicating at a high and deep level with students and parents and community members as a teacher in high schools and colleges. I had been a high school basketball and baseball coach. I had trained for the Christian ministry, with expert guidance in speaking to and in front of people. I had all the skills I needed to be really good at meeting people at the door. And Suzi taught me how to take advantage of every talent/skill I had, and to make an impact in the race by meeting voters at the door. So I learned to follow some rules:

* Never go into a gated yard if you see a dog that is unattended or unrestrained (or can't tell there is no dog in the yard) or if you see a yard sign that says, "Beware of the Dog." A voter contact is not worth the risk of mayhem. Safety first.
* Never enter a house, under any circumstances. Safety first.
* The candidate shouldn't walk alone, if at all possible. Safety first. (These first three rules may seem paranoid, but they turned out to be very good rules that everyone on the campaign trail should follow—I broke these rules periodically, of course, at my own peril)
* Always leave a piece of literature about your campaign for the voter, hopefully by putting it in their hands, or by leaving it in a place that the voter will see it and consume it later (usually in the door).
* Always remind the person to vote, about the exact date of the election and the place to vote, and about how important it is for every person to vote in every election, and in this case, especially in the primary, and especially in an "off year" election (that is, when there is no presidential election).
* Thank every voter at the door, no matter how the conversation goes, for their service at the polls by voting Democratic.
* Always make your last interaction with the voter a positive one.

When we walked for the primary, I got my sea legs and learned so much about people and what they cared about. Several people at the doors surprised me, with their depth of knowledge and understanding of the issues at hand. In many ways, canvassing can reaffirm the candidates' understanding of the larger issues at hand, and the things that impact people on a personal level.

And it shows that all Americans aren't out of touch, or merely self-consumed. Many people are thinking about bettering their communities, helping others out.

In Middletown, we met a group of African-American women living near the high school, enjoying a sunny afternoon on their front porch close to Easter. They asked me what I was running for. I handed them my walking card, a 3"×7" flier with family pictures and my story on it. They said, "We walked for Boehner last weekend, but we're voting for you! He pays $12/hour. We couldn't pass it up. But no one wanted his literature."

We all laughed, and we talked some more, and the rest of the walk we floated on air because of their interaction with us, particularly because of their generosity of spirit.

In Hamilton, we met parents at the doors who had been scared to death by the loss of loved ones and friends nearby to heroin addiction and overdose. Young people got hooked on the drug after one fix and sometimes it killed them the first time they used. Devastating. They wanted to know what I would do about the drug problem. I didn't know anything about it, really, and I know that I may have appeared to them to be just another out of touch white guy. But I listened, and offered to them that if elected, I wouldn't ignore the problem, live thousands of miles away, and have concerns that had nothing to do with the issues that citizens living in our cities dealt with every day. I would represent them. After all, Boehner hadn't come to their door in 24 years and never would. Ever. I was standing right there.

April 24, 2014

MERCER COUNTY
OX ROAST

I drove the 90 minutes to Celina for the Ox Roast. I felt very confident with our new speech, and ready to go. Marv and Katarina chatted away with me on the car ride. We talked about our lives and how we got to this spot. Both of them knew I had just finished a new book entitled *50 Christmases* (2014, Sourced Media Books) in which I detail my life story. I had planned for it to come out near the end of the campaign, and things moved right along on schedule with that project. We talked about our families, our heritage. Relaxing, good talk. We did everything we could to bury the Carney Massacre, at least in tone so far.

When we got to Celina, we easily found the venue for the event. The place seated about 300 people and they expected almost 200 Democrats to attend; the local press would be covering it. I was a big draw because of my local roots just a few miles across Grand Lake St. Marys, but Connie Pillich was big, too. Bigger really, and we realized that. We also realized that we wouldn't be able to make the Troy Forum tonight. I had accepted this invitation first after the wonderful endorsement event with the Mercer County Party's central committee on that cold, snowy night in February. We found out later that not making both events would hurt us. But tonight we focused on Mercer County.

At nearly each one of these events I found it impossible to eat much. My stomach churned with nerves. I never got over it during the entire campaign, and really, to be honest, my entire life. I had a small plate of bites of this and that (the roasted ox had become fried chicken over the years!) but not much. In the end, most of the events of this type that we worked would end and I would be so hungry afterward we had to stop for fast food on the way home and scarf down burgers and fries in the car. That's a good way to put back the hard washed pounds. Too many bad calories consumed too late at night. Tonight I didn't have much of a chance to eat anyway because the citizens who attended engaged us the entire time. Some of the patrons remembered me from my youth playing sports against teams in Mercer County (St. Marys is in the neighboring, and also very red, Auglaize County). Some were just so happy that someone was running against Boehner that they were ecstatic and enjoyed talking with us.

Others we met proved to be just flat out interesting. It felt as if the Democrats in Mercer County had become so hearty, so down to earth, so caring and kind, perhaps because they constituted the last of their kind in a place where conservatism reigned for decades now, proudly and without assault. And this isn't to say that the Mercer County Democrats were liberal. They are conservative, too. Just not the Republican kind of conservative, most of whom are one-issue, pro-life voters. I felt as though these Democrats walked through life open to new ideas, accepting of people, eager to do the right thing and make the country great, build on its strengths, provide opportunity and a step up with arms open to everyone that worked hard and those who went underserved, and those not so lucky to be blessed with motivation or who at least needed a break somewhere in life. Government can be part of that equation; and it has to be, we know that from history. Government cannot recede. That action creates less freedom, less opportunity, less possibility. These folks fought the good fight against great odds over decades filled with losing elections. My people.

Connie Pillich arrived a little later than we did because she had traveled some distance from a luncheon she had attended after attending a breakfast at even another location in this great big state in the morning. She made donor calls all day in the car. Exhausting. She had two young aides with her. They nervously said hi to us, then started working the crowd with her materials and cards and such. They had a routine they did at events and they worked the room hard.

So when it came time to start the program, the county chair welcomed everyone, and introduced me. I had prepared the introduction for her to read, which she did, having learned over time that if I didn't prepare my own introduction that I couldn't count on the audience having a sense of my whole story, important background facts I couldn't make time for in my own talk. Connie Pillich sat next to me on the podium and we chatted some. I learned about her busy day; she even looked exhausted. She patted me on the arm for good luck right before I stood up to address the crowd. Here's my opening:

> Thank you to the Mercer County Democratic Party for hosting this event, and for inviting me to speak. I am honored to be here tonight. I am running for Congress in Ohio's 8th District because John Boehner shut down the federal government for 16 days in October of 2013. As the Speaker of the House, third in line to the Presidency, he shut down the U.S. GOVERNMENT in a fit over a SETTLED LAW. He could have taken a clean vote on the budget from Day 1, and didn't. His actions, his "tactics" as he calls them, cost the American people 24 Billion Dollars. Every day that he remains in office he is hurting America. For me, from the beginning, this race has been about leadership.
>
> To me and to most Americans, leadership isn't about obstructing everything, killing government initiative, and thwarting the will of the people. Leadership is about vision, about ideas, about negotiation, about deliberation and compromise, about consensus building. These are the democratic arts of leadership and governance in the 21st C. And if you can't control your own caucus, you can't lead America. Ultimately, Americans want common sense, teamwork, and progress from their leaders, not gridlock. After all, we are all in this together.
>
> As Speaker, JOHN BOEHNER is in charge of bringing legislation to the floor for a vote. Do you think he's going to take a vote on anything that actually matters to Americans? No. His House of Representatives is not only dysfunctional right now, it is damaging our way of life. The critical issues that we are facing, the issues that if addressed would make a difference in society for the good, don't make it to the floor for a vote. Instead, we get 50 votes on the repeal of The ACA. So far, no vote on extending unemployment benefits to the long-term unemployed. So far, no vote on a comprehensive immigration bill. So far, no vote on reversing the devastating cuts of sequestration. We should be outraged about his lack of action, and show our outrage by unseating him at the polls.
>
> John Boehner has done NOTHING for America, and NOTHING for the citizens of District 8. All he has delivered is more confusion, and more gridlock.

My talk built from there, growing stronger as it went, reaching a crescendo pitch as I attacked several issues and the differences with my opponent. I nailed it. I had memorized so much of the speech that I could throw in personal thoughts that came to me or that seemed funny at the time (and this time they were funny!). The audience ate it up, and I felt like I connected with them. When I finished, they delivered a thunderous round of applause and Katarina beamed from the back row.

Now I really didn't care what Connie did, I felt so satisfied. Like I had conquered a huge mountain climb. What happened really surprised me at the time, but it shouldn't have done so given what I know now about the rigors of a statewide campaign like hers. As I sat down, Connie reached out her hand to congratulate me while the applause continued. Both the handshake and the applause were very, very nice … She acknowledged the speech's excellence with that kind gesture. Carney could have done that in Troy last week, which he didn't; but it would have been disingenuous since I stunk. But not tonight. The chair introduced Connie after acknowledging my talk and pledging to do anything she could to help us defeat Boehner. Very nice.

When Connie stood up to speak, she looked like the same old Connie, small, but powerful, and beautiful. She could take her experience and expertise to the bank, and cash in once again with a great stump speech. She owned the keynote spot, after all. But she wavered from the very beginning. She used her tablet, and got lost in the beginning, stumbling over words and telling a story completely out of order, at one point scrolling somewhat frantically to find the right spot in her talk. I sat so close to her as she spoke that I could literally feel her discomfort. One story, which I had heard her tell before fell completely flat. I couldn't tell if she left something out and it fell flat or if the story itself just didn't work this time with this crowd. She was trying to make a point about political courage, and used a story about two East German guards who had fled their posts at the Berlin wall long before its eventual fall, escaping to the freedom of the West. But the story didn't work, and the audience didn't respond. Her applause lines fell flat, even while she tried to dig her way out of it.

All the while this was going on, her aides in the back gave her hand signals, like the kind you might see if someone were trying to mimic an air force signalman on the runway. How odd. I watched them do this from the back row while she talked and wondered, "What in the world is going on? What could they be signaling?" Her speech ended, and it was good in total, but not up to par with other speeches I had heard her give.

And I realized, even pros have off nights. She had to be completely exhausted from stumping that day. Three events in 12 hours? I barely had the energy for this one event!

When the event ended, Katarina and Marv and I all hugged. We nailed it, and we did it together. Each of us had made key contributions. I felt like our campaign was growing every day, that we were getting better.

I felt like Shooter in the movie *Hoosiers* after helping the team to a big win, running the "picket fence" play for the winning shot, and then exiting the gym arm in arm with the team and coaches and the cheering crowd. From rags to riches, even if the riches proved to be short lived.

That McDonald's quarter pounder with cheese never tasted so good on the long ride home!

April 29, 2014

House Party
Here, House
Party There

For more than a month, Marv had been promising that he could deliver a house party that would make us thousands. He had Democratic friends in Oxford, all of them excited about our campaign, and all of them eager to hear what I had to say, so he said. They weren't the usual suspects that we had seen at Democratic Party events in town, either. The group was made up of different people, he claimed, mostly younger; and our common friend, a local doctor, agreed to host the party at his beautiful home. The list looked really good, if anyone would actually come to the event and write a check! If they did come, perhaps one or two of them would max out a contribution of $2,600 for the primary. We set a goal of raising $5,000 at this one event. That would be more than twice what we had made at any other fundraiser.

But we had to put off the event several times because of scheduling problems. And this caused great tension. We had already called many of the people on Marv's contact list to ask for a donation. Most had said they were waiting until the house party to give anything. So, we had to hope all of these folks would come and make a contribution or we would have to call all of them back again. We couldn't let this local money slip through our fingers. So much rode on making sure that we mined every possible contribution locally. And we knew from experience that you had to ask. Most people wouldn't just come out of the woodwork for a good cause. They had to be contacted, asked, and perhaps persuaded.

Before this event, we anticipated two more house parties the same week. Our friends in Troy, whom we had met on the campaign's first blush last November, had been planning a fundraising house party, but the tension of so many other races and candidates and events taking shape all at the same time made it impossible for them to gather a list of donors in any mass who would attend and donate. Katarina decided we wouldn't go and canceled. She determined they just hadn't put in the time necessary to make it work. How incredibly disappointing. So many people think that just anyone can post on Facebook that there will be a candidate party and that people will come. Donors/guests have to be called on the phone, invited, reminded, and called again! It's impossible to do this work easily, one contact and done ... Politics takes time and tenacity. It takes hours and many, many phone calls to pull off a successful fundraising house party.

Teacher friends had been planning another local fundraising house party for us for many months. They had vocally supported my campaign and volunteered to do a house party right before the primary. But once again, practically no one came. We thought they might be able to generate a huge turnout, maybe 50 people, mostly teachers. Ten people came, and they gave sparingly. We had fun, and I spoke extemporaneously, and answered questions. But we left the scene terribly unsatisfied and disappointed.

So we had a lot riding on the party Marv had been planning. But once again, only 10 people showed up. And they gave sparingly. We had been chasing one local gentleman who had shown interest in us, answered the phone, never responded to a hard ask, but came to this party, asked lots of questions, said he would give, then never gave a dime. We asked several people at the party, local doctors, for $500 or $1,000. We needed their help and they could do it. They gave $100 or less. We raised $750 total.

We learned that local Democrats did not participate in a culture of giving. They gave small amounts to candidates, so they didn't support my campaign at the level that a congressional campaign has to be supported. Maybe it had to do with my first time running. People may have wanted to see that I was really serious, and run again when we lost, then they would give. When I said I would likely only run once, maybe it turned people off, figuring that a one-time investment wouldn't get the donor or us anywhere. But the people who could have given and didn't kept us from reaching a fundraising figure that would let us buy television and radio ads. We could only buy print, and a few online ads. But this part of the campaign, behind the scenes, devastated us.

Even worse, the person who initially encouraged me to run and said she would do anything to support us balked time after time after time at setting up a fundraiser. When she finally agreed, she put no work into getting people to come and canceled at the last minute. I had to beg this person for a donation. She sent $50. No note. Wow …

May 4, 2014
ARMAGEDDON

The campaign had been running along somewhat smoothly for months now. At least I thought so, overall. I still felt miserable most of the time, but I tried to put things in perspective best I could, considering how busy my schedule turned out to be, constantly. The whole thing took a silent toll on everyone I loved, and on me. Chris felt neglected. She worked hard at her own job, and her best hours after work came in the early evening. I was almost always out in the evening at an event or working the phones, unless we went together to see Sam play baseball or made a special plan to eat out or stay home. So this made her grumpy, and she didn't want to spend time working on the campaign with me.

To counter how crappy I felt about spending time on the campaign and not with my family, I took the only minutes during the day that I had to myself, late afternoon around 4 pm for about half an hour, to walk our two dogs. I found a great deal of solace in this daily act. Chris and I have had many dogs over the years, but these two became the first ones that I really committed to walking each day. It brought me serenity, helped me focus on them more, and they gave me so much love each day. Sometimes they pulled at their leads and acted unruly, but they became easier to walk over time and I found a measure of peace on each walk.

Katarina jogged at this same time each day, and it helped her stay sane. But the pushing and the prodding she did, directly with me, about doing more call time, about spending more time on the campaign, all together frustrated and angered me. No amount of jogging or dog walking could keep us away from each other's throats. I said I wouldn't be a slave to the campaign, that months remained and to make it to the finish line I had to maintain a modicum of sanity by keeping merely <u>insane</u> hours, not <u>totally insane</u> hours. She didn't completely disagree with me, countering that someone who was truly committed would be totally insane, and work harder on the campaign than the staff.

Ouch.

I had been torn apart for a few weeks in particular about a conflict between the campaign and a family event. Today Sam's high school baseball team would travel with team families to a Cincinnati Reds game as part of a regional celebration of all the high school baseball teams that played in a spring tournament sponsored by the Reds, which took place at high profile playing facilities, including the Reds' own park in Cincinnati over the past month. Sam's team played at the reconstructed Crosley Field in Blue Ash in early April. It was a very cool event and game and this trip to the Reds' game was the icing on the cake. I had decided not to go today with them, instead opting to canvass and to make phone calls, only two days remained before the primary on May 6. But I could tell it broke Chris' and Sam's hearts. Everyone else's families made the trip; I couldn't or wouldn't go. I got it at home.

"It's Sam's senior year. You shouldn't miss events like this," Chris argued.

"I know, but the primary is Tuesday. Katarina staffed the office with volunteer callers, we have plans to walk to recruit voters, plus I owe her call time. I can't just <u>not</u> show up!"

"What do you owe, Sam? Nothing?"

"I owe you both everything, but I only missed one game all season, and I just can't go today." I made the decision on my own to work on the campaign today. It didn't mean it didn't hurt. I wanted to go the baseball game. I went to work on the campaign.

I complained to Katarina about this tension for several weeks. Every time I brought it up, Katarina got angry. She tested me every time we talked about commitment and effort. I believed I tried hard at everything I did in life, and that to be questioned really meant that the person was asking for a fight. Katarina never let up, until I got ugly with her.

After a couple of hours, with Chris shouldering the day and taking Sam on the outing, I broke down at headquarters. I hated spending time doing this while I should be doing something else. I didn't really mind doing the campaign work, but it conflicted!

"Come on, Poetter, it's only six months. A person can do anything for that length of time."

"Well, I hate call time. I hate almost everything about the campaign. But I am doing it, and things are going well. Why do you have to spoil this? Why can't you be happy with the progress we're making and just let me vent a little?"

"Because we need more money and because we need more votes. But all that really matters is that you make money. If you aren't doing that more, really going the extra mile, you're hurting us."

"Who is us? You work for me, remember? I set the hours. How dare you put yourself in a position to critique me. And what about me? What even matters to me at this point? What matters about my life? Look, I'm here, aren't I? I made the choice. I'm not at the game, where I should be. So lay off."

"Here we go about the Reds game again!"

We were in the middle of phone calls. We had a hundred or so calls to make and I had made 75 or so. I dialed the remaining numbers, and hung up after each first ring.

This infuriated Katarina.

"What are you doing? You didn't just hang up on her!"

"No, I didn't, but I only let it ring once. Then I hung up. I'm walking out of here today having done my part. I'm dialing all of these numbers, then I'm finished. I don't even care if we win Tuesday."

"Fine, if we do win Tuesday, it will be because of me anyway. I'm the one who organized all of the phone banks, all of the canvassing, everything. You don't even compete on Tuesday against Guyette without me!"

"That's funny. Your name isn't on the ballot. If I win, we win. You don't win, we all win. This is about all of us. And all of us are doing our part. You kill me, you know it? Yes, I should be at the Reds game today. And I didn't go. And it's the last time I don't do what I want to do when I want to do it. I don't care what the campaign costs are. That's for you to clean up after me. You have absolutely no say any longer about anything to do with my time and how I use it. All you do is clean up after me."

"Then why even have a campaign manager?"

"Exactly."

I stormed out. I didn't do anything Sunday except stew and regret that I had worked on the campaign and not gone to the game with my family. I never answered any of Katarina's calls or texts or emails all day. To this day, I'm still not over it. But things got better after this major blow up between Katarina and me, even though it wouldn't be the last one. I showed up to work on the campaign Monday, and never brought it up again. Neither did she.

May 6, 2014

The Democratic Primary Election, Winning Flat

As per Katarina's direction, the candidate is supposed to canvass all day on election day. So I started walking early and we walked and knocked on doors all day. Katarina scolded us on the phone because Marv and I took a break to pick up lunch and didn't include her, and then later I had to pick up some medical records for Sam at the dentist's office so we had a 20-minute unaccounted for time gap in our day. She made it out to be worse than Nixon's missing tapes. 20 minutes! I told Katarina it was none of her business what I did during my break times, like an employee! Another set lost!

We spent several weeks picking out the people we would invite to our victory party tonight. I made a huge mistake, thinking that a fair way to do it was to invite 1) all the volunteers who had been coming to make phone calls and who knocked on doors for us, whether they contributed a dime or not; and 2) everyone who had given money to us and lived within driving distance to attend. Of course, this list then included people I wouldn't let into my own funeral (if I had any choice about it!). I didn't think they would all come, and I didn't want only four people to show up. So we invited a large group of people to the victory party at a local restaurant and hoped for the best. Of course, several of the most critical Oxford insiders came, and stayed the whole time.

The evening went well enough, I suppose; people ate food (I paid for all of it as a campaign contribution), and talked. About 30–40 people showed up. It actually developed into a good-sized crowd. But Katarina came in late, whirling in, like a dervish, dressed flamboyantly and going around to each table wildly, welcoming friends and dissing enemies. Almost immediately she began to tangle verbally with some of the most belligerent battle axes in town, but then also with several younger supporters, including Ginger, who wanted to discuss how to get more Miami students involved in the campaign and out to vote. Katarina thought that our track record on student involvement, which had really been dismal in terms of the number and quality of volunteers (especially for phone banking), wasn't worth discussing. Neither was taking advice from political novices in the room that tried to equate winning a school levy/bond campaign with electoral politics. She dismissed them and made a few more enemies. I suppose it really didn't matter since all of these people would vote for me anyway. But the room didn't feel right all night.

We should have been celebrating, but as the results came in the election turned out to be closer than anyone thought, perhaps except for Guyette. One of the first big disappointments came when we found out that we lost Miami County. We learned later that Guyette had attended the Troy Forum on April 24 and did a really great job while I spoke in Mercer County at the Ox Roast. The Troy Forum had been televised and viewed widely in that region, and the bump he got from that probably cost me dearly there. In fact, later on in the campaign this debacle would hurt the current party chair in Miami County, when among other reported errors, party members blamed him for not showing enough support for me as the endorsed candidate in the county by paying too much attention to his own campaign for office. I never bought this argument, but we all became embroiled nonetheless as the campaign played out through October. We did win all of the rest of the counties by a little over 10% and won the night at 55%/45%. The margin turned out to be about 1,500 votes out of just over 16,000 cast in the Democratic Primary.

This was a solid victory in a square off between two newcomers/unknowns. It's the only election I'll ever win. I am indebted to all the supporters who came out and cast their vote for me. I really appreciate it and their graciousness made it possible for me to compete against Boehner in the general election. But the room felt stunningly defeated. Almost like a pall fell over the room as the evening ended. While the atmosphere should have been celebratory, I felt defensive. I stood up to give my victory speech to the group at the end of the night, thanking everyone there for their support and vowing to fight on through the next six months. But my comments fell flat. We had to get back to square one anyway tomorrow. No rest for the weary, or the wicked.

On the way out, one of my earliest supporters, who wound up giving me $500 after the win, and had run for office previously, said, "Tom, I can help you some with your victory speech."

I said, "Thanks, very generous, Hank. But you and I both know that I just gave my last victory speech." We both laughed and headed home to face the next days.

May 15, 2014

Butler County Spring Dinner, Marv's Last Stand

Headquarters settled down after the pre-primary rush of phone banking and we began to capitalize immediately on our primary win, calling donors all over the country, especially in New York and California. We also continued to cultivate Ohio donors every single day. Donors in these other states supported underdog Democrats, usually losing bids, but gave to them wholeheartedly nonetheless. And if you have the right numbers, which Katarina secured through her knowledge of the political landscape of donors nationally, through research, and by working and reworking all of the existing lists of numbers that we had, you can make money. The campaign turned around in May in terms of finance. For a small campaign, with so few employees (1), and a small group of volunteers, we had been able to win a primary, build some infrastructure for next steps, and become viable. Donors liked to hear that we had run a race already and won, and that I had something to say as a result of that race in terms of why Boehner needed to go. Donors who met me on the phone liked my background.

Now it's true that Boehner made millions of dollars during the month of May and throughout the rest of the campaign. The FEC numbers don't lie. But we competed with him, way beyond anyone's expectations, pushing our monthly total of money raised to approximately $25,000 several times. I felt like we maxed out our potential, in terms of stamina, with 21 hours of call time per week that pulled in about $6,000 per week. That gave us enough money per month and that would let us pay our salaries, add new people, keep ahead of overhead expenses, and pay for the print media that we could do for that amount (as well as buy one poll in late September). Think of the pressure that puts on everyone, though. Call time each day, those 100 calls I committed to for three hours, had to yield almost $1,000. If we didn't get any promises or actual dollars during those calls, we got really blue. When we had a great day, we celebrated, hooted, hollered, rejoiced, felt hopeful, planned new directions, made progress. There were days we made thousands and days we made zero.

But this level of progress wouldn't take us to the point where we could do TV and radio ads. It's just not enough money. To do that, we would have had to double our intake of money per month, but we worked ourselves to the bone just to make this amount. I'm very proud of the monetary goals we reached, though we fell short of making a "winning campaign" amount (@ $1 million). That's something I couldn't fix in six months. The only way to do better would be to hit the ground running like we were at this moment and do it for 18 months. I didn't have that in me, much to Katarina's chagrin. I don't think she ever believed, deep down, that I meant it when I said that I would only run once. I meant it with every fiber of my being.

Just a few days before the Butler County Spring Dinner, the biggest event of the year for the county party, we got final word that I would be speaking. This became a bone of contention between Katarina and the county chair: Nicole wouldn't invite me officially to participate until I won the primary, without actually saying that. Then when we won, she acted like, "Of course we want you to speak. You are our biggest county candidate." And all that crap. Also, the candidate for lieutenant governor would be the keynote, not me. Par for the course. I didn't care at this point. I would do everything I could to best her from the podium at the event.

All of this mostly bad news coincided with a big donor we had been trying to land coming through on the phone with a very nice contribution at the same time I watched Sammy play his last high school baseball game. The pitcher for the opponent had a great game, and Sam's team struggled. I applauded him when he made a really nice defensive play in the top of the last inning because he had six batters ahead of him with only one inning left. I soaked everything about that moment up as I watched him run off the field. It would be his last moment in high school sports, given how dominant the opposing pitcher had been.

Then, surprisingly, the opponent's pitcher unraveled in the bottom of the last inning. He still had good velocity, but he got a little wild, and with two outs he walked two batters and the hitter ahead of Sam hit a single down the left field line. Sam strolled to the plate with the bases loaded and two outs. Of course, I hoped he wouldn't make the last out of the season. I did that in my baseball playing days, and the memory still haunts me sometimes. But after a ball, and a called strike, and then a really pitiful swing and a miss at the third pitch, with the count at 1–2, Sam cranked a high fastball with the biggest swing he's ever taken to the right centerfield gap that hit the fence on one bounce and ruined the shutout. The crowd, and I, cheered wildly while his teammates roared from the dugout as Sam raced around first to second and two runners scored and celebrated, the only real excitement of the entire game. The next batter whiffed, and the teams shook hands. Sam trotted off the field, to handshakes and baseball goodbyes. What a great scene, despite the loss.

I realized at that moment that so many things had happened in those brief moments that paralleled my race. Facing a powerful opponent, flailing, but taking your swings, perhaps even connecting at points, making a difference. Not quitting! Swinging for the fences, maybe connecting here, and missing the mark there. I decided in the morning that I would write a speech about it and build several specific points of action on the story of Sam's last at bat.

I showed Katarina the draft of the speech the morning of the Dinner. She loved it. I felt inspired. I drove Marv and Katarina to the Dinner in a rainstorm. But I felt good. Inside the event, I wound up having to write a personal check to get us all in. The chair hadn't left tickets for us. This really upset Katarina. Then when we got inside the hall, she found out she got seated way in the back and not at the head table with me. She fumed and tried to get it changed and couldn't! This made it even worse. At the same time, I asked the county chair and Cindy Winter for a campaign contribution. They told me they wouldn't give me any of their personal money since I had no chance of winning.

Unequivocally, whatever relationship I had with both of them ended in that moment.

Disappointed, but undeterred, I ate a few bites of dinner, and after the announcement of a few award winners for contributions to the party, the undercard of speakers started, which I had populated many times. All of the candidates for countywide offices and a few others got up to give their short pitches. These turned out to be mostly terrible, unscripted and unrehearsed elevator talks. The crowd couldn't get excited about any of them but applauded politely. After all, this would be our ticket! Then Nicole gave me a lukewarm introduction, but ended it with a passionate plea for everyone to support me in my bid against John Boehner. "And now please welcome the next representative of District 8 in the U.S. House, Tom Poetter!"

The crowd applauded and I made my way to the podium. I thanked Nicole and gave my speech. The entire time I spoke, I felt like I couldn't care less if I did a good job or not. I saw all of the incongruities around me, the personal battles, the struggles, and just let it rip. What did I have to lose anyway? Two of the most important people in my own party didn't believe in me and wouldn't give me a cent of their own money, and made me pay my own way into the dinner. I think that letting go at this moment really helped me. I felt connected, finally, to the audience. I felt authentic and grounded telling Sam's story. The party members assembled, about 250 of them, responded, laughed, and *interacted* with me. Now this was new ground. At the end, I reiterated, "Please help us bring leadership back to District 8. I am Tom Poetter, Democrat for the U.S. House, District 8!" The hall erupted with applause. No standing ovation, but really great energy.

Nicole stood up and shook my hand and said, "Great job," and then took the microphone and said, "Wow, Tom, what a great speech. We will do everything in our power to get you elected. We are so lucky to have a candidate of your caliber running for this office." Cindy Winter even shook my hand and said, "Great speech."

"Thank you," I responded. I sat down and listened to the keynote, which came off flat and uninspired, mostly wonkish, no energy. Hope remained in the room for the governor's race, but she was there as a replacement for the candidate's original choice for lieutenant governor because of a vetting gaffe. The original choice faced immediate scrutiny for tax and debt issues in his personal finances and lasted only three weeks on the ticket. This and other revelations announced in the summer ultimately spelled doom for our candidate for governor, a really nice guy and able politician whose skeletons cost him dearly. But this night was mine. And I thought as I spoke with citizens afterward that I had reached a certain level of legitimacy with this appearance.

On balance, I recount this moment in the election cycle as my best. However, it didn't last long. On the way home in the rain, Katarina complained about where she had been seated. Then Marv asked why she had to be so negative when the night went so well. Then Katarina said that she didn't get all these Podunk people anyway, and how she wished she were back in New York City. And this really set Marv off. He had been upset about losing his place to her running call time, and felt marginalized. He let her have it.

"Maybe you should just go back to New York if you are so miserable. You're just a wannabe New Yorker anyway. Just because you lived there for a while doesn't make you a New Yorker. You're not helping anyone with your attitude."

I ganged up a bit, too, and wanted to know why she had to be so negative when the night was mine.

"I won this primary for you, Poetter!"

"I don't care. The next time you say that you won the primary, you're history."

"You can't fire me," she fumed. I knew she was right. And we drove silently in the rain for the last 15 minutes in the car, the last time we would all be together as at team.

June 10, 2014

An Angel, Heaven Sent? Cantor Loses His Primary in Virginia

Over the next few weeks, Marv drifted further away from the campaign. He stopped coming in regularly. He just basically fell out of sight. The last exchange he had with Katarina in the car after the county dinner turned ugly, by our standards, and he just felt like he couldn't co-exist with her, and certainly wouldn't take any more orders from her. I asked him to come in and do a number of different things, but his soured relationship with Katarina trumped his commitment to me. He just couldn't do it, and I had to let go of him. This meant that absolutely no one—except for a few volunteers who worked sporadically over the past several months—was left from my original pack of confidants and supporters and co-workers that started this journey. My entire original committee that imploded at my kitchen table in November of 2013? Gone. Everyone who had gotten a volunteer position with the campaign? Gone. The only person left standing? Me. No doubt, in my mind, this is the way Katarina wanted it from the moment we first met. Now she could build a staff and control the flow of people, duties, time, etc., truly a campaign manager of a campaign team she owned. From October 2013 to June 2014: A complete, total turnover in the campaign. Not one significant person on my team remained.

But I couldn't argue with what Katarina brought to the table: Knowledge, expertise, experience. Yes, she made mistakes, but so did I. I knew how good she was and how good she could be. I thought I could help her be even better.

Only she can answer if that actually happened by November 4. I like to think that during this next phase we both got better, as politicians and as people. Only history will tell that story.

As Katarina and I discussed what we would do next in terms of staffing, and as we continued to work the phones, Republican Eric Cantor, successor-wannabe to Boehner, lost his congressional primary in Virginia on June 10. We didn't even really know about it until June 11. It became such an important lever for us that we used it in almost every campaign call we made. "Anything can happen in any race! Look what happened to Cantor!" We really didn't understand what had happened to Cantor on the ground, but if rightwing politics in a "no challenger" zone like Cantor's could turn this cycle topsy-turvy, why couldn't our district turn? Given Boehner's missteps and his complete lack of presence, what if a grassroots movement to upend him took hold? We could do it if we got the support.

So we worked the phones. I was out of school, and we had no other staff, and campaigns traditionally ramp down a bit in the early summer anyway. It's too early to canvass and volunteers are on vacations and doing summer activities, not politics. So we worked the phones, and worked them hard. The goal, for me, was to make it with my sanity in tact to the July 4 weekend. We had a family wedding to celebrate that weekend, and I thought if I kept that end in mind, something joyful and beautiful, I could maintain a positive attitude through the intense call time period of post primary to July 4.

And Katarina skillfully made friends with a friend of mine, Chad Beal, who had long been interested in volunteering but didn't know how he could contribute. He didn't want to do anything with a high profile, like make phone calls, or knock on doors, and Katarina needed research on donors. Marv had balked at this assignment, and when she talked with Chad he really liked the idea, got a sample piece of work to complete from her, and excelled. Chad worked behind the scenes for months through the end of the campaign, helping us to turn the corner financially because of his excellent donor research. Chad and Katarina got along famously, like peas in a pod.

And we did have success. The Cantor loss got me through several barriers on the phone, including secretaries in the workplaces of potential donors who routinely blocked me. Sometimes the best number for a donor that we could come up with was a work number, but it rarely yielded because secretaries kept the gate, and they got paid for keeping people out. But after Cantor lost, more and more people put me through, especially on call backs. Amazing.

All I had to say was, "Hi, Jackie, my name is Tom Poetter. I'm running against John Boehner for the U.S. House Seat in Ohio's 8th District. I left a message with Mr. Jones last week to talk about supporting our campaign? Is he available to talk for just a few minutes?"

"Yes, Mr. Poetter, I'll put you right through. Best of luck in your race."

Thank you, Mr. Cantor! Once people answering the phones in the workplace for donors (doctors, lawyers, entrepreneurs, business people, etc.) got to know me, it really became just a matter of time until my messages stacked up enough that the donor knew I wouldn't give up and finally, if somewhat reluctantly, took my call. I at least got more chances to pitch my case and make a hard ask. Many of these calls yielded, in ways far beyond the basically zero chance I had of getting through before Cantor lost.

And while we raised money, we dreamed of how we would mount a ground campaign beginning in July. We knew we needed knowledgeable staffers, at least one more if not three more. Our plan became to recruit someone to coordinate voter contact. We had our eye on a local college graduate who had worked in the region on Obama's campaign in '12 but hadn't landed a full time job since his recent graduation. Katarina had used him as a volunteer, and he had all the tools, ready to go. But did he have the maturity? Could he work as hard as we would ask him to work? We chewed on this privately and gave him a few tests. He passed, and we made him an offer to join us July 1. Field Director. He accepted. What a ride he would take with us July 1–November 4! Welcome Jack Miller to the campaign!

Almost as soon as Jack joined us, we realized that we desperately needed a field organizer to be based in the Northern counties: Preble, Darke, Mercer, Miami, Clark. Jack had a friend caught between campaign jobs, a seasoned pro who had mentored him on other projects. We hired Lynn Best within days. The last person on board would be Gerald Widener. He held us off until Labor Day, but he completed our team.

Katarina, Jack, Lynn, and Gerald, and seven remarkable Miami Interns, took us to the finish line.

July 12, 2016

FALL CAMPAIGN CANVASS KICKOFF IN MIDDLETOWN

We had been planning a kickoff for canvassing both weekend days of each week through the rest of the summer with as many people as we could scare up. By September, we would be walking every day. We helped coordinate the entire county effort at knocking on doors, though it became contentious at times in terms of who would organize what routes, who would carry whose materials, who would help cover which expenses, where we would gather, who would make the organizing phone calls, etc. We finally decided we just couldn't waste time doing anything that other county operatives or anyone else wanted us to do, really. Over time, the county party kept asking us to make a contribution to the overall costs of the ground campaign for every candidate. I kept resisting, arguing that we got nothing from Nicole or from the party to push us forward. Why should we work our asses off on the phones and then spend what we raised to fight Boehner on other races? Katarina agreed, but she got pressured almost every day on the phone and email by party operatives to pony up. We could make money, and knew how, and everyone knew it now. So everybody else came to our trough to eat and drink. And they never, ever said thank you when I did relent and contribute. Not once.

Today we would have a kick off event in Middletown, meet friends from the county who volunteered to walk and carry literature all over the city for the general election, and speak with a regional newspaper's dedicated political reporter about our race. Jack had worked all week to secure the volunteers and to put the walking packets together for each canvassing team with all of the names and addresses of the voters we wanted to reach. This would be his first big project test, which he passed with flying colors. His excellence with field operations let Katarina spend more time as campaign manager, organizing from a wider view and continuing to focus on fundraising, rather than spending so much time on field operation details. We needed Jack, and especially Katarina needed Jack. He not only knew how to use all of the digital tools the party gave us to organize our voter contact approaches, but he was also just plain smart and great to be with relationally. We liked him! He provided a breath of fresh air to our work each day.

Katarina got nervous about the interview with the reporter, telling me things I shouldn't say and should say. I listened and tried to stay disciplined, but I thought that my best strategy would be to play to my strengths, be engaging, relational, and thoughtful in my responses. I thought the interview went well enough, and the ensuing story turned out to be one of the better pieces of earned media for us in the entire campaign, all the way through to the end. I have to say that this reporter gave us a fair shake, unlike some others we met and some we didn't, who painted our campaign in print as hopeless and didn't even focus on how we ran to represent Democrats, to raise issues that had been presented from only one perspective, and to serve Democracy by putting up a fight, not just conceding. At least he let me talk about the issues and produce a counterpoint to the incumbent's narrative. That turned out to be refreshing, and actually did us some good as his articles raised our regional profile as a campaign.

We showed up at the meet site early, at around 11:00 am, and met several party operatives that promised to come today. Only a few people had shown up by our start time of 11:30 am, though, and we got nervous as people strolled in late. When we finally got a significant mass of people together, about 15 on this occasion, I gave a welcome talk and turned the meeting over to Jack. He got each of the groups on the road. We spent about four hours walking and knocked on a significant number of doors with a very strong reception. One casualty, though, turned out to be one of our volunteers, who twisted his ankle getting out of his car at the first house. But he kept going, and walked his entire route. Turns out he had actually broken his ankle, and he finished the entire route. It healed by the time we saw each other for a final walk or two in October.

From that moment until now I have marveled at his courage and dedication. It finally became clear to me that we had friends in the county who would break an ankle and just keep on going. Witnessing this is very, very humbling, and wonderful, and awful all at the same time. I am so indebted to the volunteers who sacrificed their time and energy and talent to knock on doors on our behalf. What a major contribution.

And today, honestly, we really hit a stride. I felt so good walking. I felt alive, full of energy and vigor. I got so much positive feedback from friends in Middletown at the doors, mostly just impressed that we were working, were organized, and were taking on Boehner. Some people said I had great courage to do so. What I learned by the end of the day, if I didn't know it already, was that I had been surrounded by courage all along; after all, we had people on our team who would canvass on a broken ankle. That's a very powerful thing to experience and understand. And it's impossible to feel like you lost anything when that kind of sacrifice presents itself. No matter what, based on today, this campaign won, and so did the American people. This is what it's all about.

THE CLARK
COUNTY FAIR

We made a conscious decision to avoid most summer holiday parades. But I felt like we just had to participate in Oxford's July 4 parade. We did that, and I bought candy for it and got people in line to join our group to carry our banner; however, the event really had been ill conceived from a political entry standpoint. The Oxford July 4 Parade had recently been changed from a downtown parade on High Street to a parade through the community park. The thinking was that moving it to the community park would be more conducive to families participating, safer, more prone to getting people there for the fireworks show that originated from the park in the evening, etc. So we showed up and walked the route, which took about three minutes. We met very few people and felt stupid for putting so much time and money into a three-minute event. Literally, three minutes, maybe not even that! A great outcome was that Chris and the boys participated in the event with me. That was really nice, I just wish it had been a real parade.

The experience confirmed what Katarina kept preaching to us about campaign activities that fell into the category of "visibility" events. Casting a wide net didn't target voters, and didn't win votes. If you have a limited set of resources, in terms of time, personnel, and money, like we did, the only smart thing to do would be putting those resources into direct voter contact, not general visibility. Yard signs, fair appearances, parades ... All a waste of time. But we felt like we just had to do some of it. And we did.

In fact, we made it to all six county fairs in our district. It took lots of time and energy, and we enjoyed the work and the social connections, but we didn't win any votes on these trips. We did what conventional wisdom in campaigning says you should do: Show up. So we did that. I'm pretty sure in retrospect we did it mostly begrudgingly and without much gusto. But we did it.

Today we traveled to Clark County in Springfield for our first county fair experience. We appeared after Ed Fitzgerald appeared. I paid for Katarina and Jack's admission and gave them $20 to spend, just like a Dad would. Neither one of them ever had a dime, practically, the entire campaign. If they did have money, they spent it on drinks and food, in that order, and I didn't blame them at all. If I were young again and worked on a campaign, and could only find comfort in the company of booze and friends, maybe even in that order, I'd probably do it, too. Even though we paid them adequately, they were doing me a huge favor by doing any of this, really, and I appreciated them for it. I didn't mind buying them a deep-fried-chocolate-dipped-banana or fried-Twinkie-on-a-stick here and there.

At the fair's campaign tent for the Clark County Democrats, we met some familiar friends that we had been interacting with over the past few months. We also met an African-American couple charged with running the tent during our appearance that we hadn't met before, however, and they had held political office in the county as Democrats. I engaged them in deep conversation, hoping to understand more about the issues that Clark County Democrats faced, and how their leaders, especially citizens of color, saw the world taking shape in District 8.

They wanted to know where I stood on the plan for the future clean up of the Tremont City Landfill site being discussed by the state and U.S. EPA in Clark County. I knew a little about it, but asked them how it impacted the community and how I could address it on the campaign trail. They wanted to know what my plan was for reaching voters in Clark County, especially in urban Springfield, and I said that we had a field organizer, and would probably place someone in Springfield in the coming weeks and that we would walk everywhere. They liked that, and wanted to help coordinate efforts. I thought this seemed like a good direction. I learned over the next months, however, that there had been palpable tensions developing within the party in Clark, and that the party had been struggling with inter-Nicene arguments about gay marriage and other social issues during the past year, including who would organize canvassing efforts, what voters would be targeted, who would stage the routes, and who would provide the materials. Needless to say, racial divides had surfaced and I didn't have any time or much ground established to soothe these wounds. I did my best to honor the requests and ideas of those I came in contact with. But to get things done, I'm sure it appeared as though I was taking sides. I couldn't solve any of these issues, and over time became frustrated with how the players in Clark could not deliver significant volunteers to the campaign.

But our conversation turned out to be great that day, and the couple offered lodging when we made our trips to Springfield. We did not see each other again by the end of the campaign, and I never called in a favor from them. They had gotten busy, like everyone does, and focused their time and effort on more local matters. But this conversation dominated most of my time at the fair, and I thought it well spent. As it turned out, the tent drew very few newcomers. Mostly party faithful stopped by the partisan tents at the fairs. I learned that these goodwill appearances accomplished just that, establishing or renewing goodwill with the party faithful. We reached very few new voters. The events just aren't designed for that purpose. Visibility is the end game, and worth almost next to nothing.

July 21, 2014

Our Reddit.com "Ask Me Anything" (AMA)

Jack and Katarina worked themselves into a tizzy over their success at getting an AMA session for the campaign on Reddit.com. The sessions are called AMAs for "Ask Me Anything," I told them I had no idea what that even is, "What's a Reddit?" They, of course, found my response to be completely lame and insane, completely out-of-touch, which it is, but I just didn't know. I found out quickly that Reddit is a longstanding online community that—among many other digital functions—periodically hosts press conferences through a question/answer format, usually for famous people. Subscribers enter the press conference and ask questions about anything! Literally anything. The responder gives responses as he or she sees fit. The session lasts for as long as the host says it will. In this case, I told Jack and Katarina that I thought I could give it two hours. They wanted more time, but I thought the format would be exhausting and if we did well we could always get invited back!

The idea is to be honest, and thorough, and genuine when answering questions. We spent some time talking about how we would answer the questions. We decided that once the press conference started, I would decide which questions to answer and write relatively short responses to as many as possible. If we all felt a topic just didn't merit a response or we didn't want to go there, we would just ignore the question. This can be perilous, but it's an option. And, after all, you can't answer all of the questions if there are a lot of participants, which we found out to be the case; our AMA turned out to be highly rated! Both Jack and Katarina had to approve my response word for word or it didn't post. We answered the questions we thought we could give a reasonably strong answer to, and skipped all others without regret.

The first thrill for Jack and Katarina came in getting a spot in the queue for this event with Reddit in the first place. Celebrities usually get AMA spots on Reddit. But Jack and Katarina had applied for one on a whim and got a spot! Reddit liked the idea of Boehner's challenger getting a shot to meet this part of the public (and Boehner would never do anything like this himself!). Jack and Katarina also hoped that there might be a fundraising bump for us, that those who participated in the session might consider donating to the campaign. The session posed an opportunity for "visibility" that they actually liked because they thought it would raise our profile and maybe even raise money.

I must say that the event turned out to be exhilarating, thrilling even, especially for Jack and Katarina. Just think, hundreds or thousands of people gather on line to ask questions and read answers. Then they respond to your answers, creating layers of dialogue! The event exhausted us. We never could have gone more than two hours and stayed sharp enough to keep going: a two-hour press conference is long. We worked the whole time, thinking and writing and arguing and posting for two hours straight. What I learned was that I could never give a completely satisfactory response to any question, to either the easy or the difficult ones. Members would jump right in and question my answer, or give their answer, or a better answer, and pull other members in for their responses. I felt like the doctoral candidate at a dissertation defense who doesn't really have to do any defending once the faculty start discussing and arguing amongst themselves! Easy street. That's exactly what the Reddit members did! They questioned, we posted, they chimed in with their two cents, we moved on! Priceless.

We thought the event turned out great and we celebrated it even though we also got some stinging criticism from participants! Moreover, though, we felt a sense of camaraderie as a team that we hadn't felt yet in our work together. That turned out to be a nice outcome. Also, we made a few dollars as some respondents made small donations. But the best outcome turned out to be an email Katarina received from a colleague who had been asked by people from a prominent Washington politician's staff which media group we had hired to answer our questions during the AMA! They saw it and thought they would contact our media group and give them an interview to represent them!

Our media group? Right: a candidate with a PhD in education and no political experience, running a "service" campaign against an unbeatable foe; a college educated, first-time campaign manager, focusing mainly on finance; and a field director in the second week of his first job out of college. What a team. We probably should have quit the campaign at that moment and sold ourselves as the next great political media team and relocated to Washington!

BUTLER
COUNTY FAIR

I was excited about meeting Ed Fitzgerald again at the Butler County Fair Friday night. There had been a little friction over our appearance, though. Ed and his people didn't care if we came and met them and campaigned together. The more the merrier. When the county folks heard about it, though, they weren't pleased. We learned that they wanted their own county candidates to get all the attention with our next governor at the event, and would rather I come at another time. But we couldn't really go to the fair at any other time. I insisted on appearing. They relented. They couldn't keep me away anyway. It's a free country, after all. I can go to the fair anytime I want!

Jack and I drove over together. I hadn't let him drive since he almost got us all killed trying to merge onto State Route 4 from 73 East in Middletown on the way to a canvass. I found out on that trip that he didn't know how to merge, and both he and Katarina thought it patronizing that I offered to teach him how to drive. I said it was a matter of experience with merging and just took supervised practice, that's all. They argued that I thought my way was the only way, shoving it down his throat. Well, merging is a pretty specific skill with very particular steps. I wanted to help, and I didn't want to get killed before offering it. The result turned out to be Jack never drove again, and he still didn't know how to merge. Funny thing, we got excited talking about a topic on the ride over and I wound up exceeding the speed limit and got pulled over by a state trooper.

"Where you going tonight, Sir?" the patrolman asked.

"We have a campaign appearance tonight at the fairgrounds. We got to talking and I lost track of my speed. We drive this road all the time. I'm sorry."

"Well, I'm going to have to give you a ticket. You were going too fast for this stretch and you need to pay better attention."

"Yes sir."

Crap! I hate it when the campaign manager's right! I shouldn't be driving. But my designated driver has to know how to drive, at least how to merge! But at least he probably wouldn't be speeding!

We didn't mention the mishap to Katarina or Chris. They both would have freaked out! More money out of pocket, and the possibility of compromising the campaign!

When we got to Hamilton, cars backed up for half a mile just to get into the parking lot for Friday night's festivities. Smash Up Derby headlined. When we got to the tent, we met everyone just ahead of Mr. Fitzgerald. He had been on the road all day and was ending his run with this appearance. We gathered at the tent, while a barker from the party announced my appearance to applause of those gathered, more than 50 by now. That would be the biggest crowd for a political appearance that I saw at a county fair all summer. We handed out buttons and fliers and talked with everyone we could. When Ed arrived, we welcomed him with applause. Neither he nor I gave a talk; we just greeted people and talked with them one-on-one. We had a blast.

Just a few minutes into the session, the notorious Sheriff Richard Jones, world renowned for his right-wing positions on immigration and crime, showed up dressed to the nine's in his full Sheriff get-up, the smoky bear hat, the dress uniform, the whole nine yards! He has an impressive, commanding presence. No doubt.

I walked up to him and said, "Hello, Sheriff Jones, I'm Tom Poetter. I'm running against Boehner this Fall."

"I know who you are, young man. Say, I've really scared the crap out of you Democrats with my positions on immigration, haven't I?"

His bluntness, rudeness amazed me.

"Yes, very scary. It would be great to talk with you more about it, but I don't want to ruin the mood of the event."

"Sure thing, I have a lot of people to check in with here."

I stuck out my hand and he shook it. I said, "Nice to meet you, Sir."

"Same here."

Crazy. He bounced around talking and carousing with all the Democrats he could. I guess he was the next governor's security that night. We laughed about that later, how ironic.

In a quiet moment before Ed got back on his bus, I asked him how he was doing, personally. He couldn't resist giving a campaign response before opening up a bit.

"We're close, Tom. The polls show the race with Kasich at 43/41. So many undecided voters. We are making great progress. Kasich knows we can win. But I'm tired. This is grueling. Sometimes I don't even know where I am. But anyone can do it for a short period of time. We can win this race."

"I agree. Great job tonight. Thanks for being so kind to me and my staff and for making us feel part of something bigger. Be well and enjoy your trip."

"Good luck, Tom, nice to see you tonight."

Everyone said goodbyes and we dispersed. Great event.

On the way home, I asked Jack if he had ever been to a county fair.

"Nope, first time. What's a Smash Up Derby?"

I had more teaching to do beyond merging, as well as a speeding ticket left to pay!

July 30, 2014
TROY CAMPAIGN HEADQUARTERS KICK OFF

The state party decided to invest in the infrastructure for an elaborate call center in Troy for Dee Gillis, running for a state senate seat against incumbent Republican, Bill Beagle. The party thought the incumbent's seat was vulnerable, and that a win there would eliminate the super majority that the Republicans enjoyed in the state house. So they put an internet-based, Voice Over Internet Protocol (VOIP) system call center in an office with 10 computers in downtown Troy. The idea was to staff it and inundate the region with phone calls for Dee Gillis, both in terms of voter contact and fundraising. I'm not sure they ever really got the system off the ground over the course of the next three months, but it was impressive. I wish we could have gotten that kind of attention, but it was nice to be included in the Miami County headquarters kick off. We got invited to the event and accepted the offer right away. We drove up to Troy after call time.

When we got there around 6 pm, just a few people had shown up. We had gotten there about an hour early. So we waited around. Someone went out to get something to eat, then we ate, talked, and interacted with our Miami County friends. This turned out to be really important to the campaign, this time just relaxing and waiting around for something to happen. Because when the room got full, we all took our turns as candidates saying something about our campaigns and how much Miami County's support meant to us. I went last, as the federal candidate, and really enjoyed speaking from the heart about all of the great people and relationships that had been built between our campaign and local Democrats.

This event proved to be pivotal, since we would rely on locals for so much support in putting together canvasses and phone calls. The event cemented our commitment to Miami County and our connection to the headquarters in Troy. Katarina got a key to the new headquarters, with an invitation to use it as a hosting site for any activities we wanted to do. It turned out not to be the most convenient location to use, but the gesture was tremendous. We felt like we had friends and colleagues that valued us and "saw" us tonight. That meant a lot to us.

DAYTON IRONWORKERS ENDORSEMENT MEETING

To be honest, until I met our friends in the Dayton Ironworkers Union I really didn't understand what unions do for themselves, their members, and society. Katarina and I got invited, after the tremendous efforts of our friend from Eaton in Preble County, Sam Strong, who had been working on our behalf canvassing and encouraging us from a distance. He got us the meeting with the membership tonight, and thought that ultimately the union would be able to make a contribution to our campaign, which they did.

We arrived long enough before the actual members' meeting to get a tour of the union facility. It is tucked on a piece of property in Dayton, with a nice parking lot. It's a low rise building made of brick, just one story above ground. I found out right away that the union owned the building outright, and had recently paid off the mortgage. They were very proud of that. Inside, on the right, were the offices. On the left was a meeting room large enough for 100 people. The basement housed a huge training facility where the member-teachers gave lectures and demonstrations for old and new union ironworkers on safety and the latest techniques on the job. Sam had been serving as a union teacher for the past several years. He told us about the classes, how they are taught, how much education the members commit to, and how much they pay in dues.

"Wow, everyone pays the same amount in to the union, no matter the pay grade?"

"Right," said Sam, "You show your commitment to the job and the organization by working for a good wage, developing a network of friends and co-learners, and building a career in ironwork. When you get where we are, veterans, the sacrifice pays off in a strong pension. And we commit ourselves to getting the best and brightest workers in this union. When they are good, they work. And when they make money and build strong, they make us look good. And we continue to get hired, and the coffers grow. We are the best workers in the world—well-trained, smart, eager, responsive, tough, and good. We can pay for our own space, for our own continuing education, and for our own pensions. We are all in this together, and we're independent. Our hard work leads to freedom. This is one of the most democratic institutions in America: made up of workers who represent themselves, represent each other, elect their own leaders, work hard, reinvest in ourselves and the nation. This is what it's all about. This is why Democrats love unions, and unions love Democrats. We believe in the same things. Ultimately, businesses hire us to do the job right the first time, and to save them money. We never redo anything we start; we get it right the first time."

This speech almost made me cry. Sam, by far, understood the world, hard work, sacrifice, and how to care about things that actually matter way more deeply than I ever would. The truth is, America is great because unions are great. And here we saw the proof in the pudding, up close and personal.

After the tour, the union leaders invited me to say a few words. I had been watching the union members drag themselves in to the 6:30 pm meeting. They had been working all day. Some of them had to stay after the meeting for several hours for a learning session with Sam. Then they would be right back at work at 6am. So I knew I couldn't speak long. I had prepared the following remarks, which I gave quickly. I shook as many of the members' hands as I could on the way out. I did my thing, fully knowing that not all of the members were Democrats, and knowing that they probably hated me a little bit, just another politician asking for money. But they treated me great, and I told them I admired them, and respected them, and promised to fight for them as hard as I could if I got elected to represent all the citizens of District 8, including all of the ironworkers from the counties in District 8 that worked out of this union shop.

Thank you to Ironworkers Local and to the members and leadership for the Invitation tonight. Thanks especially to Sam Strong for his interest in and support for our campaign.

I want to thank you specifically for the commitments you make every day to good-paying jobs, to protecting collective bargaining, to worker training and re-training, to work place safety, and ultimately, to the pursuit of the American Dream—doing productive work every day and achieving economic security. I guarantee that if elected I will serve you by protecting these commitments, and doing everything in my power to strengthen them.

I got in this race in October of 2013 because of the government shutdown and because of Boehner's complete lack of leadership in our district.

I want to return to a pursuit of the Democratic arts, exercising skills that the Speaker doesn't have, by: Listening, Developing ideas, Building consensus, Negotiating, and Compromising. We need solutions to our biggest problems, not stalemates, inaction, and outright obstruction.

This race can only be won by turning voters. Direct voter contact is where we can make the biggest difference. This means many volunteers knocking on doors, running phone banks. This is an important election, from the top of the ticket down. Thank you for helping us during this last 90 days to get out the vote and to make a difference.

Tonight I am seeking your support, both in terms of an endorsement and financially. I pledge, in turn, to support your work and enterprise. Thank you for supporting candidates and Democratic causes. I am Tom Poetter, Democratic candidate for the U.S. House, District 8. Thank you from the bottom of my heart for your efforts in building a great America, and for your hospitality tonight. Godspeed.

They gave me a polite round of applause and ushered me out. I was never in my life so proud to be an American citizen as I was in that moment.

August 6, 2014

DARKE COUNTY
DEMOCRATIC
PICNIC

The end of the summer ushered in the full-blown campaign season. People took their last gasp vacations, sure, but by August 1, most people had started back to their regular activities. If they were prone to political activity, now was the time to ramp it up. Events stacked up, night after night. After so many events, and with so much going on at headquarters every day—including call time, call banks, canvassing planning, and actual canvassing runs—we didn't spend any time at all preparing for events—planning what I would say, what we would do. When we got in the car, we had usually spent the entire day campaigning already, so summer days on the campaign trail turned out to be really long. When we piled into the car for the Darke County picnic, we knew that we would be meeting most of the same people we had met on the campaign trail already in Darke County, and that probably nothing new, no major breakthroughs, would happen. But we went, and we went willingly, though the 60-mile drive weighed heavily on us.

I drove, of course, and Jack and Katarina relived the day from the backseat. We had just gotten word that a political mess had started brewing in Butler County, a potential strike by the county social workers over a lack of substantial raises and workload issues. I told Jack and Katarina that I thought that we shouldn't get involved, that a federal candidate wouldn't get into the weeds over a government employee work issue at the county level. Boehner would never get involved in something like this. He would trust the county officeholders at that level and allow them to do their work. He might advise if called in, but that would be a rare occurrence. Of course, the Republicans certainly didn't position themselves as "pro-union," and more accurately you would say that their typical words and actions on union issues would position them as "anti-union." So, there might be some benefit to getting involved in the conversation about the strike and the issues at hand from a Democratic perspective. To me it would be getting into the weeds. But Oxford operatives had begun calling us, asking us to take a position, and to support the union side. Both Katarina and Jack agreed that we wouldn't get involved. There would be consequences to this decision, almost immediate ones.

When we got to the picnic late in the afternoon, around 5:30 pm, the sun had yet to go down and still blared down on Greenville. The thermometer still raged over 90 degrees, and sweat just poured out of us. No one could stay dry in that heat. This made it hard to eat; all we wanted to do was drink lemonade! So we talked to everyone we could, an even older crowd than we expected, and worked with the "tech crew" while they set up the microphone for the talks. Thing was, the microphone was set down about 18 inches below the concrete slab for the shelter house, at the far end of the edifice. So I wouldn't be standing in at 5'7", instead I could have a foot and a half deficit to deal with. The party members listening to tonight's speeches would see me as 4' tall. I had seen just about everything so far, so I didn't even think twice about it. But it proved awkward giving my speech.

I gave the same baseball speech that I had given at the May party dinner in Hamilton that killed. But I couldn't generate any interest. As I think about that night, I don't know that anyone could have gotten that crowd excited about politics in that heat. I know that people came out that night at about 30 strong because they had always come out for this event, and wouldn't have missed it as part of their summer routine, no matter the heat and no matter the speakers.

By the end of the night, we had ourselves locked in to visit Darke County one more time for its famous county fair. The members wanted us to come on the night celebrating military families. The Darke County Fair is known across the state as the best there is. Big grandstand, lots of acts, great attendance, etc. A Smash Up Derby. We would appear one more time that month. We hoped we wouldn't burn up at the fair like we did tonight. We had now kicked into survival mode. More days, more events. We knew none of it meant more votes, but we knew we were campaigning, learning the ropes, connecting with friends.

August 7, 2014
CLARK COUNTY
KICK OFF

Clark had been stoked about their headquarters kick off for weeks. They thought that they could get quite a few volunteers out to their new headquarters to hear from local candidates, and me, at 6 pm. They boasted that they could have a rally, which contrary to popular opinion, is very, very difficult to organize and pull off. Candidates need star power to pull off a rally. If there is no star power, then organizing is the only way to get a rally to actually happen. It takes hundreds of calls, and then plenty of luck with the weather. We looked forward to the event, and knew that we had a chance to make a good impression, coordinating friends together in Clark with our new field operative, Lynn Best, Jack's friend and mentor that we had hired to help us on the ground in Clark and Miami counties, in particular.

We left way too early for the event, scheduled for 6 pm. Our 4 pm departure gave us a hefty two hours to get to the new headquarters in Springfield. The trip only took 90 minutes, routinely. But wouldn't you know it? Just east of Dayton we ran into a huge snaggle of cars backed up on the highway for miles. We couldn't get around it; we were just stuck. We found out later that an accident blocked the road for quite a long time, backing up traffic for miles. And even if we had gotten off the highway, we still would have been hard pressed to find our way to the location on back roads. We toughed it out on the highway; basically waited the traffic jam out. We stayed in touch with our friends at headquarters, but we didn't get there until 6:15 and they didn't hold the start of the meeting. The rally took place right at 6 pm and we missed many, many people who came and went before we could arrive. Our friends there were hugely disappointed, but gave me a chance to address everyone that remained, practically as soon as we walked in. About 20 people remained from the approximately 50 people that gathered. Why the rest left so quickly, I'll never be able to fathom it.

I told the group remaining how sorry we were about being late, that we had made it a campaign hallmark to be on time. I mentioned that me showing up 15 minutes late could never compare to John Boehner NEVER showing *up before, now,* or *ever* to talk with citizens of Clark County, let alone address their problems. I started to get their attention. I gave them a few applause lines from my stump speech, and left it at that. The mood changed in the office, and we spent about an hour discussing field strategy with the operatives who stayed behind to talk politics and to work with other campaign hands representing other races in the county and region. We met several other candidates, and renewed a few old acquaintances from earlier meetings, and then I got embroiled in the controversy at hand.

The fact continued to be that the factions of political action groups, mainly splitting across racial lines, vied for my attention and trust. No matter what I said or what I did, there was nothing that my campaign could do to broker the tensions that existed among the competing groups. Over time, we simply tried our best to work with everyone, canvassing with as many leaders as we could when we walked the grid and met Democrats at the doors in Springfield. Over the next few months, walking in Springfield became a wonderful pleasure. The people there embraced me and encouraged me. And I had a chance to meet up with my first cousin from Columbus, Linda Sohner, who walked with me on several weekends over the next few months.

I'm sorry we showed up late that night. I'm sorry that traffic created havoc. I wish I didn't have to win people over every time I showed up somewhere. But I'm glad that the people in Clark County welcomed me, gave me a chance to speak, and worked so hard on my behalf for the next several months. This fact would always be persuasive and constant to me throughout the race: Boehner would never show up because he didn't have to and because he didn't care at all about the citizens in Clark County, in Darke County, in Mercer, in Miami. He took his strongholds for granted, and if he ever did anything in the District, as opposed to Washington or for the National

Republican Party, his efforts would be focused on Butler County. But I found out that the citizens, in terms of the way they voted and how their partisan allegiances lined up, didn't care. They didn't want a representative, it seemed to me. If they did, they wouldn't re-elect someone over and over again who didn't care about them and made absolutely no effort on their behalf.

HAMILTON
CANVASS

I loved walking in Hamilton, knocking on doors. The thing I loved most about it is that citizens really engaged us at the door. In some cases they poured their hearts out about the issues they had with living in the 21st century in a society that undervalued them. In other cases they rejoiced that someone taking on Boehner had knocked on their door and asked THEM what they thought needed changing in Butler County and in Ohio and in the nation. Further, they displayed hospitality and warmth that resounded with us as genuine, deep, and real. I got invited into numerous homes, and in the end, I had a very hard time resisting the invitations.

On our walks in Hamilton in August I met the following people, among so many others:

I knocked on the door of a small, but nicely decorated house, with white wooden siding and a well tended yard, with the front door open so I could see the expanse of the home inside. A young Black male in his late teens came to the door, greeted us warmly, and we told him who we were and what we wanted. I handed him my door card and he studied it. After we talked politely for a few moments he said, "I think my great grandma would like to meet you, come in."

He opened the door for us. I hesitated a second looking back at Jack, but relented when he just shrugged his shoulders. So I left Jack at the door and I entered the house. My new friend led me back through the house, winding through the kitchen, the house surprisingly deep, and to his great grandmother's bedroom in the back. She lay in bed, motionless. I thought she looked to be in her late 70s or early 80s, obviously infirm, still in bed in the late afternoon. A young girl, no doubt her great granddaughter, lay at the foot of the bed on top of the covers caressing her great grandmother's arm. When her great grandson spoke, he said quietly, "Granny Marie, this is Tom Poetter. He's our Democrat running against Boehner for congress. You wanna say hi to him? He came all the way from Oxford to say hi to you."

She looked up at me, her eyes glassy and mostly vacant, but with a stirring voice said, "Let me look at you," she took my hand and pulled me closer. "Yes, run against Boehner. Beat him, son. Fight to the last measure. Don't let him intimidate you. God bless you for coming to my house."

This burst of words, lucid, passionate, took a lot out of her. She held onto my hand, but let me fall back to a seated position on the bed, then when she relaxed back into bed, I stood as I let go and thanked her for welcoming me into her home and for raising her great grandson and great grand daughter so well.

"They are good children. And Louis, he's a good boy. And so are you …"

Her voice trailed off and I let her go. Her great grandson escorted me out, and I asked him to make sure she voted. He said she always voted absentee ballot since she couldn't make it to early voting or the polls anymore.

Jack said, "What happened back there?"

I said, "I just met the greatest living American citizen. A national treasure. Great Grandma Marie."

Jack looked at his list and put his head down, making his way to the next house.

I had just learned again in that moment why I walked the streets.

Later we came to a group of larger housing units that looked like several houses that had been joined together by "new" construction. It was an older domicile, not really contemporary, but the complex architecture of all three buildings together made it rather impressive. We had three female names on our list for this address, all of them with the same last name. We had to squeeze our car into a vacant space on a side street, since most of the street was parked up.

We knocked at several of the doors, but to no avail. The place felt and looked vacant of people, though not "unlived in." As we walked back to the car, a Black male in his mid 30s pulled up behind us, and he got out of the car quickly, and asked with some agitation, "Who are you guys? What do you want with my aunts?"

"I'm Tom Poetter. (I handed him my walking card) I'm running for congress against Boehner. I just won the Democratic primary last month. We were hoping to speak to the women at this address about voting."

His demeanor shifted very quickly; his eyes sparkled and he shook our hands vigorously.

"Sorry for the gruff greeting. My aunts live at this address and they are away. I'm taking care of the houses for them. It's a little disconcerting seeing white guys poking around the place in our neighborhood, as you can imagine. I'm a schoolteacher, and very interested in your race against Boehner. Tell me more about what you are doing."

We talked with Marcus for an hour on the street. We learned so much about him, his family, his work, his students, and the state of the community in Hamilton. Several weeks later, my new friend walked another route with us in another part of town, solidifying his support for our campaign and cementing our friendship. I had no idea that I would make lifelong friends knocking on doors for a campaign.

At one of the last doors we knocked on in Hamilton tonight we met Miss Priscilla, a former elected official who lived in Hamilton her whole life. She looked to be in her late 60s, very vital, full of vim and vigor. She spoke as though she had seen Hamilton built from scratch through the late 1900s. She told us some of the history of her home, how long she had lived there and why she worked so hard to keep it in good order in terms of curb appeal, and on the inside economical to keep it cool, warm, and an enjoyable place live. Her pride in her home and community just overflowed from her. We enjoyed speaking with her, and learned a lot about Hamilton that we didn't know.

"Just remember," she said, "A lot of people have blazed a trail for you to win some votes in Hamilton. We are going to do the very best we can on the ground, through word of mouth, mainly, to help you. What I want you to know is that it's so good to see a candidate at the door. God bless you, Thomas."

"Thank you, Ma'am," I said, and Jack and I both tried to shake her hand. But she would have none of it, embracing us both with big hugs, and sending us on our way.

Jack and I looked at each other in that knowing way, like we had just had a day to end all days on this campaign.

"I love the people of Hamilton," I said, as we drove back to home turf.

Miami and Mercer County Fairs

Jack and I embarked on a daylong jaunt to two county fairs: the first, in the early morning to Troy (Miami County) and the second, in the late afternoon to Celina (Mercer County). We had to leave Oxford at about 10:30 am, arriving in Troy around noon. We met our contact person from the county party, Lilah, at the Democratic tent. A couple we had met at another event would watch the tent while Lilah and I walked around passing out literature and talking about the campaign. We walked the entire fairgrounds, and spoke with about 20 people. Sparse crowd, very overcast skies, a rainy day. On the way back to the tent, I decided to say hello to the Republican women watching the tent right next door.

They greeted me warmly at the start, welcoming me, showing me their literature. Then I said, "You know, I don't want to keep this from you. I'm Tom Poetter from Oxford. I'm running against Boehner for the U.S. House seat."

They stopped dead in their tracks. Went completely mum. Then I said, "Well, look, I didn't want to ruin your day. I just wanted to say hi since we're right next door here, and after all, we're really all on the same team."

One of the women mustered up her courage and said, with her lips quivering, "You know you have no chance."

I said, "I know, I would be crazy to think I could win. But then isn't Democracy at least about running, about presenting an alternative point of view, about giving citizens a choice? No one ran on our side in '12. It's time that Boehner had a real challenger."

And now the second host weighed in, "Well, God bless you Tom Poetter, what with the first class whipping Boehner is going to give you in November." She didn't say it with a smile, but with a thinly veiled malice.

I didn't mind the jab, I just chuckled and said, "Nice to meet you ladies. See you at the polls."

I heard them twittering as I walked away. I gathered up Jack at the tent and he asked, "What were you doing next door?"

I said, "Just making new friends, Jack. You know me, never met a stranger."

We got in the car and made it all the way to my hometown of St. Marys before grabbing a bite to eat. I insisted on stopping at Lee's Famous Recipe Fried Chicken, one of my favorite old haunts in town. The chicken is great, and we ate and talked and laughed about the day so far, consuming way too much chicken, way too many mashed potatoes and fresh yeasty rolls. I felt free today to be myself, with call time suspended for a day while Katarina took the day off to attend to some personal matters. So she sent us boys on the county fair trips; she really hated visibility events and wanted no part of them anyway. Fine with me! It helped us all for Katarina and me to have a day off from each other here and there. No harm done.

We arrived in Celina at around 5 pm, our appointed arrival time with the county party, and found the Fairgrounds easily. When we walked up to the Democrats' tent, a crowd of 15–20 friends that we had been cultivating in the party since February met us and congratulated us. They really appreciated us coming to visit and rolled out the red carpet. They had a great tent, with water and snacks and shade, as the day had turned warmer and sunnier late in the afternoon. One of the members that we met at the party meeting in February, Mel, pulled people from the midway to meet me, dragging them to the tent, telling them that I would be the new representative if he could get enough Mercer County people to see the light and get rid of that bane, Boehner! I interacted with many, many people, including those who didn't mind getting into some verbal fisticuffs with Mel and me. Our Mercer County friend always diffused the tension with a backhanded compliment or a comment about a family member that put the debaters at ease. I never had to wade out of the muck; he always did that for me. Several people got heated with us, but he loved it and the entire mood remained jovial and fun.

As we prepared to leave after a couple of hours of greeting people and talking, one of the members brought an older gentleman up to me and said, "Tom, this is one of our oldest party members, Ed Johnson. He wants to share something with you."

"Tom," Ed said, "I'm so happy you are running against Boehner. He just flat out has to go. One thing I'm hoping you'll do is set the record straight about our true American history. Have you read my flier?"

He handed me a flier entitled, "The Truth About Supposed Moon Landing." I skimmed it quickly, and laughed, pointing out the funny lines about how Hollywood had staged the moon landing in California, just as it had Glenn's orbit and other events in the 60s and 70s. I had seen these fliers before, which had always been presented as a joke.

"Ed, come on, this is hilarious. How did you come up with this?"

"Well, it's all true," he said, and I could tell that I had hurt his feelings.

"Oh ... You really don't think the moon landing happened? Really?"

"No sir, filmed in Hollywood. Propaganda, all of it."

Then the member who had introduced us yelled over, "Hey, Ed, get over here and bring me one of those fliers! I've got another live one here!"

The member winked at me as he bailed me out of the set up.

The Mercer County Democrats—lively, funny, smart, generous, cantankerous, old school, conservative—turned out to be the most wonderful, engaging Democrats I met on the campaign trail, as a group, all summer. They helped me beat Guyette in the primary 219 to 154 (59/41). But we only mustered 721 total votes in the entire county to Boehner's 4,816 in November. A bloodbath. Nothing I could ever do could ever help me create a home field advantage in Mercer County. I might as well have lived a million miles away and grown up on Mars. However, from a personal perspective, in terms of lasting, memorable, inspirational attempts, efforts, and against-all-odds, true-believer support, worn on the sleeve for all in the public to view, the Mercer County Democrats ruled. I loved them. These are great people, all 721 of them, a true communion of saints crying in the wilderness.

Inside County Politics, Losing on the Strike

Yesterday we heard from Burt, our old campaign friend, regarding his plan for involving us in the county social worker strike. Our staff talked about it again, and we agreed that we couldn't and wouldn't get involved in it. But Burt insisted, writing an email "inviting" us, basically giving us an ultimatum, that we should attend a scheduled rally for the workers tonight in order to guarantee his ongoing support and that of other prominent progressives in the county.

I agonized over this, then dug in, keeping my head down, not bowing to the lowest common denominator for a campaign by chasing publicity or notoriety or approval. I definitely wouldn't respond to ultimatums or threats. To me, presenting an ultimatum meant the end of a relationship. I would negotiate, but I would not get painted into a corner. So, I thought I had to trust my instincts and my principles. I felt very strongly that the social workers had been treated poorly in our county, and that they had every right to strike. I also thought that they had very little chance of succeeding with the strike since the other public employee unions in the county had already settled, giving in on salary and merit pay issues in ways that the commissioners applied to the social workers' case; as a result, the county officials would have no choice but to bring in substitutes to keep services going. No one wins when this happens, especially families.

I also felt as though the process had to work itself out, and that outside influences may inflame certain powerful entities and actually keep both the workers and the government officials from moving forward. I also thought that if I were elected to the U.S. House, that I would NEVER get involved in any way, shape, or form in local matters in a manner that would upstage the elected officials in charge of the issue or problem. I might work behind the scenes, but never publicly by taking a side. That just wouldn't happen. I feel as though that kind of action is a recipe for disaster, and would encourage no open dialogue, no public trust. I don't think elected officials at the federal level usually do take stances like this and inflame duly elected public officials struggling to reach agreements on local matters. And certainly candidates don't do this, at least the ones that think that if they are elected that they will represent everyone in the public.

I also felt that if I did get elected, I would have to make complex, difficult decisions based on my principles and the political climate. And I knew that I would do popular and unpopular things that not everyone would understand or support. Knowing that to be the absolute truth of any future situation, I had to deal with the fact that I might make decisions that my own supporters didn't agree with. And if my own "strong" supporters didn't agree with me, and if they would leave me and not support me further as a result of one decision on one issue, if they would desert me on a whim as in this case, then so be it.

This is the position I settled myself into, and I lived with the consequences. The matter wouldn't be resolved by the election, and it hung over our heads. The strikers went back to work without a deal on September 9, and the dispute, with a new contract in place, didn't get resolved until April of 2015! The fact of the matter, politically, is that I probably committed a major misstep from the very beginning. I should have written a supportive letter and showed up to support the social workers at the very beginning, and then supported them online. I could have done this, minimally, and avoided any unrest or disregard inside the party. I just didn't think I should.

And then I felt attacked for no reason when I didn't go along and I got angry. I'm still angry. I thought to myself, "So this is how it's going to be? I can play that way. If you don't care about my perspective, and just want to threaten me with pulling your support, and I know I'm right not to proceed, then I would have to learn to live with my positions, and the outcomes!"

This is something most people never experience because they don't have jobs that put them in a position to make decisions that have a profound impact on others. In a way, this was a very important test for me, which I passed, in my opinion. Politically, I lost some ground. But if I were to be elected to serve all of the citizens of District 8, I couldn't just jump when someone said "Jump," especially if my feet were cemented to the ground. I wasn't going to jump. I'm glad, in retrospect, that I lost in this case. I learned a lot about myself, and I don't think I hurt anyone, maybe excluding Burt and myself. If anything, this experience got me ready to govern more than any other experience during the campaign.

August 16, 2014

Headquarters
Kick Off
Canvass

With the controversy about the strike hanging over our heads, and the summer heating up with canvasses and call time to donors and call banks designed to contact voters, we thought that we should try to reinvigorate our Oxford base by hosting a Fall Campaign Kick Off Canvass event at our headquarters. Truthfully, we needed more local volunteers, and Katarina had been mostly unsuccessful at drawing our old volunteers—who had been so helpful during the primary campaign—back to the general election campaign. And she had trouble pulling in new volunteers, with so few people available, and so many local candidates to support with get out the vote efforts.

Ultimately, today's lackluster event led Jack to pull out all the stops to recruit a new cohort of intern volunteers from Miami. If we couldn't draw a host of consistent volunteers to the headquarters to make phone calls or to walk with us throughout the district, maybe, Jack thought, he could get some of his former professors at Miami to sponsor campaign internships through their departments for students interested in committing to an intensive 10-week congressional campaign, essentially September 1 through November 4. His goal was to recruit seven new interns to the campaign, and put them to work phone banking and knocking on doors, constantly. In just a few weeks, he had commitments from professors, and he had begun contacting prospective interns and interviewing them. Jack had seven new interns in place by Labor Day, and they carried us through the Fall. More about their amazing work comes in the closing pages of this book.

But today for our headquarters' kick off (which had actually been open for eight months!) we invited everyone we knew for an 11:30 am luncheon and rally at the offices. We hoped to have 50 people, and to send them out on walking tours throughout the county. But by 11:45 am we only had 15 people, mostly diehards. We invited our friend Sam Strong from Eaton to introduce me and during his talk he handed us a sizeable check from the Ironworkers Local. Wow!

Yet this event, like so many others, no matter how hard we worked, turned out to be so much less than what we planned, or expected, the check notwithstanding! The rule of thumb turned out to be that we would almost always be disappointed, no matter how much we tempered our expectations for support. It almost never went the other way, meaning, a throng never appeared out of nowhere to sweep us up in its passion and enthusiasm. That just doesn't happen on campaigns, usually, and it never happened to us! And almost every time we thought we would draw a crowd, I would work myself up in expectation for it, hoping that we would finally see some real excitement for the campaign manifest in a strong turnout.

During my short speech welcoming our volunteers, I joked that our goal at the doors in the county was to introduce our campaign to people who probably had never heard of us, and not necessarily to get embroiled in political debates with people. I said, "There are many times that we don't even like politics around here. There is so much other work to do!" And I said it tongue-in-cheek, at least half-jokingly, perhaps letting my guard down a little bit with friends. But our old friend Larry Barr, who had been at our earliest campaign meetings, a formerly trusted now mostly defunct friend of the campaign who came today for whatever inexplicable reason, said to me after the party, "I really didn't appreciate that remark you made: 'we don't even like politics.' Why are you even in this race if you don't like politics? It doesn't make sense." Berating me, browbeating me, at my own party.

I couldn't even respond to him; I walked away without answering. Amazingly rude, both his question and my walking away. For me, personally, in that moment I decided I didn't want to be remembered as the long-shot candidate who punched a "supporter" in the face and went to prison for felonious assault. I didn't want that, and I thought it could have happened in that moment if we exchanged any more words.

I went to the restroom, waited for the room to clear, and walked out with four people to canvass with. We had hoped for 50; 15 came to the party; 4 people walked. Needless to say, Larry Barr didn't walk. I guess he was too into "politics" to do that!

The few, the mighty … Poetter for Congress! Off we went! To canvass, not to jail.

August 17, 2014

SPRINGFIELD CANVASS

We determined to walk in Springfield even if our organizer on the ground in Clark County struggled to get rival factions together to support us. Several other local candidates commandeered volunteers that we tried to recruit, and finding new people in the party to walk proved to be a nearly impossible task. So, we showed up and walked, all of the staff from Oxford, as well as my cousin Linda from Columbus. Whoever else joined us, joined us. But this Sunday, as well as several other Sundays in the Fall, we devoted to Springfield. When we looked at the map and considered the population and studied voting patterns, we determined that Springfield could be a place where we could pick up a significant number of votes. The way to make sure voters supported you? Contact them at the door.

I enjoyed walking in Springfield. The people we met at the doors invigorated us. They cheered for us, and laughed with us, and talked with us at the doors about their lives and the things that they wanted to see a representative do for them and the district. When I walked with my cousin Linda, I had the pleasure of reconnecting with one of my 15 or so first cousins, who was a little more than 10 years my senior. My mom and dad had kids late; almost all of my first cousins were much older. She's just one of a smattering of Democrats in our family. Most turned Republican long ago, I don't know how or why.

When we went to the doors in Springfield, Linda would introduce me to voters and often say at the end of the conversation, "My cousin is the most honest person I've ever met. You can trust him. He won't let you down." Every time she said this I felt so lucky, and just a little embarrassed. She put her emotions and feelings out there for the public to hear and I really appreciated it. This reconnection meant so much to me and strengthened my resolve to walk, and talk, and serve. Thank you, Linda.

August 20, 2014

THE DARKE COUNTY FAIR

The Big Daddy of all Ohio county fairs is "The 'Great' Darke County Fair." Maybe it's the best county fair in the nation; it's debatable. I knew this fact about how great the Darke County Fair could be each year while growing up in St. Marys, just an hour to the north. But I never attended it as a child. We always went to the Auglaize County Fair, just a few of them over the years really. I never had any personal business at the fairs, no overwhelming draw of friends showing animals at the fairs or people to see in neighboring towns. This changed a little when I got to be a teenager. I went to the Auglaize County Fair and walked around for fun every couple of years or so. But I would have to say that I'm no real big fan of fairs, or rides. I do like the food, and sometimes, the rush of the crowd. Tonight, in Greenville, we felt the rush of the crowd.

We met several candidates from the district, including Dee Gillis, who had her staff members with her and along with us worked the grounds talking to everyone we could who stopped by the tent. Dee and I shared some time together and I always enjoyed her friendship and experience and warmth, and tonight would be no exception. As a long time politician, she had been elected several times as Mayor of Tipp City, a Republican stronghold. She and her husband Kelly brought a great deal of know-how and genuine care to the stump. He had been the Chair of the Miami County Democrats for many years. But, we knew that Darke County would yield practically no votes, no matter what we did. Even if people liked me, we knew they wouldn't vote for me. People just didn't vote Democratic in Darke County. Our research over several elections showed very little movement in the number of Democrats registered and/or voting in the county, numbers so low as to make you cry or give up if our daily goings-on didn't at least give the impression of competence, if not growing strength.

But tonight the fair hopped with an undeniable energy. Like at the Butler County Fair earlier, a Smash Up Derby was the key event later in the evening, and a salute to military personnel day continued, and several big animal sales and/or contests were going on. The fair packed the grounds with people, visiting tents, exhibits, and events. And they flocked in to the Democratic tent—friends and neighbors, and some voters, no doubt, but deep down, just good ole' country folk at the fair, down home, real, engaging.

Some of the guests had no intention of voting for us; some were eager to connect with us and encourage us on in our race. We met most of the citizens at the tent, but the group spilled out into the midway, and we had fun talking with people, engaging voters in the hustle and bustle of the moment. When you think back about joyful moments in a campaign, with everything humming, and people getting along, these moments stand out. The signs, the buttons, the colors, the smells, the warmth, the energy, the people—the sheer magic of it … sticks with you. It makes you appreciate how few people in the world get to do this, to feel this way, to engage people on the ground as a federal candidate. In this place where practically no votes lurked, we thrived. The Darke County Democrats put us into a position to be our best, interacting with voters. And the trappings of our shared Americana filled us with hope, and joy, and wonder. What a great moment.

We had a great day on the phones, too, before the trip to the fair. By this time, with just 10 weeks to go until election day, our call time hummed along, and we had begun making headway now for several weeks in terms of money raised. People knew this was happening, that we were spending time on the phones, and that the results had turned for us. We had money to spend; not enough for media, but enough to get our message out with a staff and through print.

On the ride home, Katarina and Jack, my team, whooped it up and celebrated the day and the night. We had come so far, and now we had nothing but sprinting left to do. The pace would pick up considerably. Katarina warned me about this, but I really didn't get it until I found myself in the midst of the whirlwind.

SAM'S COLLEGE "MOVE-IN" DAY

While the campaign hummed along, I got ready to go back to school, but not before moving my son Sammy into his freshman residence hall at Miami University. I had been a wreck already about this for several weeks. I had lamented Mitch going off to school two years earlier, and it hurt a lot because I missed him so much, but I had Sam in reserve for two years, still living at home. Now it was time to send him off, too, creating the inevitable, and very real, empty nest. I wasn't ready for it. Some parents live for it. Me? Just the opposite. I dreaded it because I knew the gaping hole that would be left. That doesn't mean that I didn't love Chris and that I thought we would be bored or lonely without the boys. The truth is that I really, really love both boys to heartache and love spending time with them. I just didn't want to give that up. I wasn't ready. I suppose most parents aren't ready, no matter how they posture or what they say to the contrary. But the day came just the same; I couldn't hold it off.

I remember most of it as a blur. Getting out of bed, going through the motions, showering, getting Sam out of bed, eating breakfast, all the while holding back the emotions, trying to keep an even keel. When we got the car packed, we drove in and had a very easy time, really, unloading. We had tears saying goodbye but didn't sob. No one had to be dragged kicking and screaming to the car. We didn't have any big emotional blow-ups over nothing, either. Sam really did a nice job of moving us along. Later around noon as Chris and I discussed what to do next with the rest of our lives, Sam texted and said, "Could you guys pick me up for lunch? Nothing is being served and the guys already went with their parents."

"YESSSSSS!!!!" we wrote back. "Be right there!"

What a tremendous reprieve. We raced back to campus, fighting traffic, but we didn't care. We picked up our boy, and took Sammy for lunch, and soaked him up. It felt like weeks since we had seen him. It had only been about 90 minutes! So much to talk about, so many dreams and experiences to hatch, to have, to create, to savor, to dive into. College! To this day, I remember that lunch like it was yesterday. I recommend it to every parent: Move your kid into college, leave, and take him or her to lunch 90 minutes later. What a joy!

Our parting after lunch went so much better. We love that boy.

Both boys played such a huge role in my campaign, by being great sons, by loving me, by playing ping pong or pool with me in the basement, by talking about sports, by taking me out to eat, by asking me how the campaign was going, and how their favorite player in it, Katarina, was holding up. What a joy.

I didn't work on the campaign today. I worked on life, instead, and am so glad I took the opportunity to do so.

The time at the end of the day helped me get ready for my own classes, and to jumpstart a new way of doing business with the staff. Going back to work meant fewer hours on task during the day, several nights a week out for classes, and more evening events canvassing, phone banking, and dialing for dollars. The time crunch set in, and I couldn't do anything about it. What I did have going for me that I can never replicate or coach anyone into was a loving family, a great wife, and two wonderful sons. All of that remained the case, no matter what else happened to me. After all, I learned, my family really didn't care about the campaign at all. They cared about me. That's the truth, and the joy of it all, especially looking back.

My Last "Big" Speech in Oxford

With school starting up, and Labor Day, we spent most of our campaign time on the phones, phone banking and dialing for dollars. The campaign slowed down a little bit with outside appearances for a week or so before heating back up. Our next big event would be my last speech in Oxford, an invited speech for the local Democrats at their quarterly meeting. I spent some time writing a new speech, a sort of thank you to locals and a plea for volunteers.

In the background lurked the social workers' strike still looming over the county. I told my staff members that I couldn't be trusted not to bust a gasket if I got questioned in public about it, especially tonight, and especially if the audience waded muck deep into it with me. I wouldn't have it, and would bury anyone who brought it up, "it" being my seeming neglect of the issue, under a scathing barrage of epithets and sailor-like swearing. I just didn't care anymore. We had been through so much and I just wouldn't put up with any crap. Katarina and Jack knew I would never actually do it, but I could tell they felt edgy, too, about this last invited speech of the campaign in Oxford and my agitated state. I would give many other talks before the finish line, but this would be my last moment in front of the locals.

I realize that this sounds like I didn't care about the social workers in our county, or the families they serve, or the local Democrats who supported me. I did care then, and I do care now. Deeply. I just didn't think I could help the social workers' cause any by making appearances on their behalf. And once the locals started laying down ultimatums, I dug in my heels. On the backside of things, I realize that no one in the union cared what I did or thought it would make any difference. No one from the union ever contacted me. But to me, the issue brought me to the brink of "hard decisions," and I paid a price for it internally, and of course, with Oxford "friends" who thought I let them and the union down. Politics.

Tonight, after working on the phones for several hours, I showed up as late as I possibly could to the event. The space filled with the regular people I had seen at events and parties for almost a year. No new faces. I spoke for about 10 minutes to about 50 supporters. Here's a sampling of what I said. I got personal with the crowd and asked for their full support:

> So can a staff of four full-time, excellent staffers and a candidate win? No, they can't win it alone. Money is one thing. A paid staff is great. Paying a staff and funding a robust direct voter campaign are important. But this staff has to be able to recruit volunteers to threaten, and to win. Nothing happens without citizens manning phone banks and knocking on doors. These are the lifeblood of any grassroots political campaign. So, you have to say yes to a request to phone bank, or canvass. If everyone in this room gives 10 hours along with a friend or a relative they recruit, then we can make a difference. Don't leave it to this staff to run and to work their fingers to the bone and to fail, without helping them! Reward them by saying "yes!" when they call you on the phone to volunteer, and make a difference on the ground doing the purposeful work that matters, turning votes … . Political change in this country is made by small increments of work done by people who believe. Campaigns of our size, structure, and goals rely on volunteers and friends and we need you now.
>
> I want to tell you all something. We are running a legitimate, Democratic congressional campaign for the first time in this district in a long time. What we are doing has truly never been attempted before. We have a laser like focus on our purposes. We have assembled a first rate, full time, paid staff. Work with them.
>
> I want this campaign to be a testament to people who step up in impossible circumstances. I want this campaign to honor the progressive ideas that we all share, and to honor a belief in democracy. I want this campaign to be a testament to the people who do this for the love of it, and not really for the money, but for the hope embedded in winning, and serving.
>
> Remember in 2012 when you went into the voting booth and there was no one on that ballot contesting Speaker Boehner? This isn't that year, and I am so proud, and so excited, and so happy to be doing this. This is worthy work, and it's hard and it's exhilarating. But together we can make a difference.

We have enough money right now to compete, but not to win. Will you help us? We have a strong staff that is knowledgeable and committed, but they don't have enough help. Will you help them? We already know that Boehner is canvassing and phone banking and polling for the first time in a long, long time, from the May primary through today. Will you make a difference? Will you truly join us? Do you have the courage, to come full circle, to buy in to the purposes of this campaign, to compete, to dream, to help, to run, and maybe even to win?

I will answer that question for the final 60 days by doing my best to represent you on the campaign trail. How will you answer it? Will you simply say, "Yes"?

I am Tom Poetter, Candidate for the U.S. House, Ohio's 8th District.

I stepped away from the podium to a rousing round of applause. The county chair, who never gave us a dime, was there and said to me during the applause, "Maybe this won't be your last speech in Oxford. Maybe you'll be right back here giving a victory speech in November." I said over the din just so she could hear, "This is definitely my last speech in Oxford."

I turned and waved to everyone one last time before sitting down. I exchanged pleasantries with the patrons in that room for several minutes afterward, until the room cleared. Not one person wrote a check that night or after; just a few stalwarts volunteered in the eight weeks to come. I knew I had their votes, but I couldn't get them to work for us.

September 10, 2014

Local Teacher Union Event, A Complete Waste of Time

I really can't blame one of the largest teachers' unions in Southwest Ohio for what happened tonight, but I want to report how dicey and maddening campaign events can get for candidates, especially considering the fact that practically no one showed up for the event, except candidates, and the format changed at the last minute without any warning.

The event was pitched as a "meet and greet"; no speeches would be given. So we didn't prepare anything to say at all. When we arrived, the host said to all of the candidates assembled—over 40 of us from many, many local and larger races in the region—that we would each have two minutes to speak. Of course, that meant that the speeches would go way longer than that, which they did, and the host would do nothing to control the rambling, which she didn't. It also meant that there would be a free-for-all for the microphone, since she gave no order for speakers. You walked up and took the microphone and grabbed it away from the previous speaker to get your two minutes, or you didn't, a kind of Darwinesque, political freak show. And guess how many teachers came to the event? Wait for it … eight! That's right, eight teachers, with more than 40 candidates in attendance.

I steamed and fumed and tried to walk out. But Katarina wouldn't have it. She actually caught me in the parking lot after I bolted for the car.

"Where are you going?"

"I'm out of here! This isn't even what the event was supposed to be. It's a meet and greet. And now we have to stay and listen to 40 speeches? Why stay? There are eight voters in there, and we don't even know if they live in District 8! Talk about a waste of time. A complete and total loss! A freak show to beat all freak shows. I hate this campaign!"

"Get back in here! There's no walking away from this. We committed the time and we're here. We had a good day on the phones. Just relax … and keep your voice down."

Katarina telling me to "just relax" or to "keep my voice down" really struck a nerve, since I felt as though I was the one constantly trying to settle her down, talking her off the ledge. Irony of ironies: someone telling me to keep it together? So, I exploded.

"No … way! Got it? I'm not going back in there. It's a freak show, for eight people," I seethed, surely foaming at the mouth by now.

"Just say a few words about our race and we'll go home," she smiled at me and seemed nearly genuine. I think she liked that I was into it, fully pissed off, taking ownership. Despite the daily madness and the bickering, I realized how much Katarina cared for the race, and for everyone working the campaign.

I must have looked at her as though she had just landed in a space ship and walked out of it down one of those impossibly shiny metal ramps, speaking rationally, in perfect English. Who was this person?

I laughed hideously. The whole thing a nightmare, no one ever doing what they said they would do, constantly shifting, making mincemeat out of any plans that you would make. Insanity.

So, I went back in, and gave a completely lame 1-minute talk about my race against Boehner. I led with, "I don't suspect that any of you have heard of my opponent, the speaker of the house, John Boehner?" A laugh line. Crickets. Not one of the eight people even looked up at me, their heads buried in plates loaded with cheese and crackers. It went downhill from there. We got out of there with practically no dignity in tact and this infamous set of lines that I uttered over and over, perhaps yelled, all the way home in the car, "That's the last event where people change the format on me. I won't put up with it. I'm walking out next time. These things take time, and energy, and focus to prepare for. No one just walks in and does it (of course they actually do)! Crap!"

And so ends another glorious day on the campaign trail against the most powerful politician in the opposition party. Nearly complete malaise.

TV Tapings, Free "Earned" Media

The summer days turned fall-like, and during these crisp, new days we started to feel the impact that the Miami interns, all seven of them, would make to the campaign. Jack had them sign up for specific hours to work on specific tasks. Every day the interns devoted a significant number of hours to phone banking and knocking on doors. We traveled in small groups all over the district in the afternoons and evenings to introduce people to our campaign. They spent hours on the phone making hundreds of calls to voters asking them to support us at the polls. In just a short few days, the interns picked up the pace at headquarters, complemented our existing volunteers, and brought life and energy and hope to our work each day. They worked so hard, they always showed up, they listened and learned and contributed. Several times they lifted me up with their innocent, thoughtful energy, their amazing enthusiasm, their insights, their knowledge. Most people think I'm an enthusiastic person, but I was getting tired at this point. But students, youthful people, the young, have a way of lifting you up, helping you see the goal line, which, of course, is right in front of your nose, that is the political process yielding new interactions, new relationships, new experiences, and new ways of viewing the world and each other in productive ways that better the world, in the moment.

In the end, interacting with the interns, feeding on their energy, connecting with the deep commitments they made to us and to the democratic process, reconfirmed all of our hopes and dreams on this doomed campaign.

Jack did a masterful job of recruiting them, scheduling them, coaching them, and befriending and including them. After awhile, Katarina, very skeptical and distrusting that the students would actually make a difference, became their second biggest fan. I will always be their biggest fan. What a tremendous job they did, what a tremendous sacrifice they made, literally on my behalf, but also for democracy and our futures as well. These are great citizens, who would become even greater citizens. I'm so proud and grateful we had a small amount to do with that transformation. In fact, we feel as though we got more than we ever gave.

As our days shot toward election day, several area TV stations extended the invitation to all campaigns at the state and federal levels to come in for a two-minute stump speech taping which they would post on their websites and show on TV at a designated time before the election. We couldn't turn down this type of free media, so we got my elevator speech down to the allotted time, and made our rounds. At the first station, we got the royal treatment, escorted to the production floor by assistants who greeted us at the door, assigned two engineers to do the taping, and a very short window of opportunity to get it right, about 15 minutes. You could do as many takes as you wanted in your allotted time, but the station would only use a complete take, they would do no editing. If you messed it up, you had to start all over from scratch.

I decided to take a first crack at it without my notes, attempting to do what I had not ever been able to do in any other type of situation with visual media in the past, that is speak into a camera eloquently for any length of time, producing something that I'd actually want people to look at and listen to. This is really, really hard to do without a script. But I gave it a try, twice. Both takes went along fine, then I got lost or flubbed a word and couldn't recover, just like you see on outtakes of any show. So now I had to go back to my script, which I read into the camera, looking down as little as I had to, and looking into the camera as much as I could without losing my place. I drew on all of the speaking training that I had gotten over the years and the experience of putting it to use in front of classes and small crowds, and got it right on the first try. It really came out quite good, and despite having to read it, we felt pretty good about it. People in the region saw it, and liked it. I wish I could have done more media like this and got it out to thousands of viewers. That may have made a difference, perhaps not.

On the way out, the director said very kindly, "Don't worry about reading it, Tom. It came out great. We have only had a few people here who could do that without notes and get an acceptable take. Yesterday, John Patrick Carney came in and did his in one take. Best I've ever seen. Okay, take care now."

Of course. No massacre today, but a reminder of how strong the talent pool in politics is, in our own party.

At the second station, similar rules applied but we were able to send my script ahead of time and they loaded it into the teleprompter for me. They ran my script and I could look into the camera and read/interpret it without being tied to the paper, looking down. This helped tremendously, and after getting used to the teleprompter (it would be my first and last time using one!), I got the best take on the second reading. We left the station very happy with the outcome, and feeling like we would make a good impression if anyone saw the digital shorts at the website or when they would be televised more widely by the stations.

On the car ride home, Katarina said, "Nice job, today, Poetter. That went really, really well. I wish we could get you out there more. You're good, and getting better."

That was a really nice compliment, and I needed it. As she spoke, I really appreciated her comments and said, "Thanks, Kat. Great day today. None of this happens without you. Great job." We rode the rest of the way home mostly in silence. As we drove, I thought about all the missed opportunities that today revealed. We couldn't afford high production quality video media, or commercial time to air anything even if we could afford to put it together. We couldn't get TV stations to cover our campaign (except one that did a really nice 90 second piece on the campaign in mid October). We didn't take the time or put in the effort to make videos of me for YouTube. We missed opportunities here, but we did it consciously. We really had to take advantage of today's TV opportunities, but the work became an important football for us that we stopped kicking around early on: media is hard to control, it doesn't target voters. If we waste time and money on it, it might make us look competent, but it's still a waste of time, meaning it won't actually move voters. So we concentrated our time and effort on direct voter contact strategies—phone banking and canvassing. I know it was the right decision. But the best campaign would be one where you could do both, and live with the consequences. The ingredients needed for that approach? More time, more money, more expertise. We ran short on all of these most valuable commodities. By the time we knew how much we missed the mark, it was time to vote.

September 19, 2014

RIVER BEND
COMMUNITY TRIP

We used Labor Day as a short "catch your breath" period a few weeks back to take stock of what we needed to do in terms of personnel changes as we moved into the campaign's final two months. We all decided we needed to hire our friend and volunteer, Gerald Widener—who had been around Butler County politics, Presidential politics, and our campaign from way back in October of 2013—to run call time and take over finance. He could do it, we knew it, and had been recruiting him to join us full time for months. Finally, he relented. We made him a strong financial offer, and we said he would run call time, be in charge of it. He saw it as a good opportunity, better than his part time job; he saw the progress we had made, and he wanted to commit. We all benefited from him joining us full time through Election Day.

Getting Gerald on board full time, of course, lightened the load around the office. Having his expertise with the voter database tools, and especially his practical experience in the field as a political operative over several campaigns in the region—which came into play and strengthened our thinking and strategizing—really benefited everyone. He could do anything we gave him to do, and he did it all well, just like Jack had done from his very first day in July. In the end, hiring Gerald and having Jack on hand with 10 weeks of experience gave Katarina the ability to step away from the almost completely time consuming activity of running call time and raising money and allowed her to take the campaign home in the final 10 weeks. She could oversee everything now, with staff in place, as a true campaign manager. Katarina and

I really needed a break from each other, too, to be honest. The three hours a day that we had spent together since March doing call time had taken a toll. We did well, but we couldn't keep it going. We both needed new direction, new challenges on a daily basis. So Gerald saved us, renewed us.

And he volunteered at the end of his third week to go with me to River Bend, a retirement community in the county with a "strong" Democratic group of about 30 people who met monthly to talk politics and support candidates. The leaders of the group had been to several events during the campaign, and invited us early on (in May) to be a speaker at their September gathering. We gladly accepted. I didn't spend a lot of time preparing for the event, by this time I thought about a few issues I would surface, a few comments about Boehner's lack of effectiveness, especially about how he had deserted us for Washington, and take questions. Gerald acted pleased to be in charge of me for the night. We left early, got there early, greeted new friends, and welcomed the other guest speaker, a woman in her first race for a county office. She was really nervous, and we tried to put her at ease. But nothing except being finished with her talk would cure her. Jack and Katarina stayed behind to run phone banks and to go out early for a weekend night. They deserved an evening off.

The host asked if I wanted to speak first or second after dinner. I knew that my colleague desperately wanted this to be over so I said I would go second. This proved to be a great relief to her, and made her able to choke down a small sandwich and a few chips before our talks. After dinner, and a short introduction by our host, the candidate stood up and gave a very nice heart-filled talk about her first race for public office, what she had learned along the way in the short run so far, and how much she appreciated the support of the people in that room. I thought she did a great job, and praised her extensively when I stood up to speak.

I said, "I've known Grace for two months now. We have walked together in your city, and knocked on doors, and met citizens. She is a terrific candidate, with excellent experience and a strong platform. She deserves your vote, and I hope you'll convince as many people as you know that we need her in office."

I turned to her and gave her a round of applause while the rest of the audience joined me in another round for her. It was heartfelt, but I could tell I really touched Gerald, who beamed in the back. He saw me taking shape as a candidate, growing bigger than myself, connecting with voters, letting my best qualities come out. Not trying too hard, trying just enough. Not stretching for approval, but demanding it with my words and actions at every turn. Taking people I met seriously, listening to them, being part of a bigger team. Running to win America, and a few votes and hearts and minds in this room, though I really didn't have to try that hard. They would vote for me if I face planted into the potato salad on my plate and then gave my whole speech covered in food, mumbling through the crumbs. But I became a candidate nonetheless, and it mattered to me, and to those closest to me. I had wanted so desperately to get here. Tonight, more than any other to date, I arrived. And it felt good.

Folks listened to my talk, which came out without a glitch tonight. I had passion, a few funny lines, and at the end a few people asked questions. Not too long, not too short. Trying to keep things going, our host asked one of the guests, who he introduced as "our resident politician," if he had any comment to make, and he said, after a pregnant pause, "I'm flabbergasted."

Everyone laughed, but I didn't know what that meant. I smiled and said, "Sir, what do you mean by 'flabbergasted'? If I've been unclear or upset you, give me a chance to make it right."

He said, "That's it. I'm flabbergasted."

I said, "So be it."

One of the strangest moments in politics I've ever had. But I just kept moving. Sometimes people just melt down. Maybe he wasn't feeling well. I don't know. I just know that it was a great night.

When we got in the car, Gerald jumped at it, "What was the deal with that 'flabbergasted' line? You kicked ass tonight. Great job."

"Thanks, Gerald," I said. No doubt, without question, a great night. "I don't know, no matter what any one person says or does, it can't ruin what we know. I am the best candidate for this job, and I should win. Maybe the guy thought he'd never live to see the day when the Democrats could put someone up who was smart, funny, personable, and connected to them. Maybe he never thought he'd see the day when we could win. You know, we could win this thing. We could."

Gerald smiled and said, "Well, even if we get our asses kicked in November, we will always have River Bend."

"Absolutely," I said, and we joked and crabbed and yucked it up all the way home. A great night for our campaign, and for me, and for Gerald, the flabbergasted notwithstanding.

September 27, 2014

CULTURE FEST, SPRINGFIELD

We devoted the entire day Saturday to Springfield. The city hosted a cultural fest—an uptown fair celebrating diversity and community action in the City of Springfield—and we had been invited by the county's Democratic party leaders to come and meet people at their tent and enjoy the day with as many Clark County citizens as possible. We planned on leaving late morning, taking all of the interns and entire staff, and meeting friends at the Clark County headquarters, visiting the culture fest for two hours, like between 12–2 pm, then knocking on doors the rest of the afternoon before calling it a day. Lynn, our field director for Clark, could make it, of course, along with Katarina, Jack, Gerald, and me, along with five of the interns. We piled into two cars, made it to Springfield before noon, and campaigned at the culture fair for several hours.

Our crew fanned out and talked to people, handing them buttons and fliers and asking for their votes. When citizens found out I was there in person, the crew brought them to me and we talked about whatever was on their minds. We had a steady flow of people from the event and people just walking up to us for two hours, non-stop. When things died down a little in mid-afternoon with the heat soaring, we got in our cars after saying our goodbyes, and hit the streets. We knocked on hundreds of doors through the dinner hour.

Exhausted, we picked up our walking groups and headed back to Oxford. We stopped for a quick drive thru sandwich on the way home, and I bought the students' meals. I couldn't stand to see them spend a dime of their own money after all that they had given that day. What an effort they made. Yes, they were getting internship credit for the work, but they had to pay for that, too! They deserved more than we could give them, so feeding them made sense. And they were so appreciative, so wonderful.

We realized that the interns loved us, and quickly became devoted to our cause and to us. In a sense, they chose us, too. So the energy was there from the beginning. They grew in their political acumen, understanding better what the issues are and how to talk about them, and they learned techniques for campaigning on the ground with the staff and the candidate. And we valued them, and they sensed that. Their efforts made a difference. They quickly became part of our team and made us strong, impressive. We showed up with 10 people, and made a good splash. And then we knocked on so many doors, that even the young people among us faded at the end. I got really tired, but by this time in the campaign, I had dropped my weight to 170 pounds. I could walk for miles without fatigue, or water, or a restroom stop! I felt great, and strong, and able. I may never feel better for another day in my life than I felt this day in Springfield, Ohio.

POLL RESULTS

For two weeks we had been fighting as a team about conducting our own poll. We knew Boehner had been polling because moles had been reporting to us for weeks that they had gotten poll calls from his campaign, and this raised a significant flag of awareness, especially as Boehner fought perception problems at home, as distant and ineffective, and more broadly on a national level, as incapable of building consensus, on the one hand, and for standing up (or not) to the radical conservative caucus that saw him as wishy-washy. So Katarina had begun discussing the idea of hiring a polling company to conduct a poll, and I resisted it vehemently. Everyone, especially Katarina, knew how tight our budget looked through November. We had contracted with The Jackson Team to do a series of really great print mailings to hundreds of thousands of voters. That didn't come cheap. The financial and design commitment had already been mapped out with The Jackson Team, and Katarina had been working hard on putting the mail campaign together, plus we had overhead expenses that wouldn't stop for anything, and the salaries that we had added. So I had to keep making money on the phone, and each day the pressure mounted to produce during call time.

Katarina argued that we could use a poll that came out favorably to our benefit by telling donors we had gotten close to Boehner, within striking distance. That would be the critical lever for donors, and the lack of polling had actually dogged us throughout the campaign. I tried to convince people we could win on the phone, and some donors gave to us because they believed in us and believed in the process. They surely didn't think we could actually win. But some potential donors wanted more data, more proof that we were at least competitive before donating. In response to Katarina's argument, I said that the money and time it would take made a poll a bad investment. We wouldn't really have enough time to take advantage of positive numbers, and what if the poll confirmed what I already thought: That we faced an insurmountable gap, which for me made an open and shut case not to fund a wild goose chase?

Then Jack joined the fray. They usually didn't pile up on me, but this time Jack tagged in. He got right up in my grill, pulling his chair on wheels as close as he could get to mine, and said, "Tom, we have the money. I looked at the books. This is going to cost $3,000, maybe a little more, I don't know. But this is a good price, and the polling company is a really good one, recommended by The Jackson Team. It's going to be worth it. I think we are doing better than anyone thinks we are. Our work is making a difference. Let's prove it either way. If we don't like the results, we'll just keep our heads down to the finish line. No harm done."

Katarina beamed at the doorframe, so proud of Jack making his case to me, standing right on the threshold, neither in or out of the room.

She said, "Poetter, come on, even Jack thinks it's a good idea. And you know how conservative he is." Which he isn't, of course, far from it, and we all laughed.

Then I un-spoke a big, deep, pregnant pause on purpose, probably for five seconds or so, and sighed deeply, and finally said, "Fine. Do the damn poll. $3,000, that's it. Not one dollar more, and if I find out you spent a dollar more than that, I'm firing both your asses on the spot. And if you come to me and say that the poll shows us down forty points, then I'll say, 'I told you so! And now we're down three grand for absolutely no reason!' and fire both your asses on the spot. The … damn … spot! Got it?"

They both laughed, and ran down the corridor, immediately hitting the phones to set up the poll. I smiled, and went to lunch by myself while they played. I brought them sandwiches and soda pop. I was as popular as ever at HQ.

We carried on for a few days, business as usual, except for the extra time Katarina and Jack spent working with the pollsters, and then all of a sudden, it seemed, Katarina stood at the door after taking a call and just grinned like a cat and said, "Poetter, you are not going to believe this. That was the polling company with the results. First, the poll puts Boehner at 46%. That's incredibly low for a sitting Speaker of the House. And when the pollsters read your bio to prospective voters, you poll at 38%. 38%!!! Can you believe that? We have to get on the phones right now!"

And we did. We called back every single caller whom we had talked to for six months who said, "I can't give you anything until I know you're close. I need poll numbers first."

We had our best day ever on the phones. We made thousands of dollars in just a few hours. Katarina and Jack beamed. They had been right, really right. And I praised them, "You guys? Wow. Great job. Wonderful, excellent work. I'm so proud of you."

Then they told me it was me, that I was a great candidate, that I deserved to win, that they believed in me. That felt so good, I can't even describe it. It meant a lot to me to have the staff in such a good position coming down the home stretch.

We held on to this "win" for weeks and weeks. At every turn we mentioned Boehner polling at under 50%, at 46%. Of course, we learned later that the results of this poll wouldn't have any predictive power for how people would actually vote on November 4. People would vote for their party's nominee, not me. And this would lead to devastating results. But for now, the political impact of Boehner's low polling helped us immensely. It gave us hope, and energy, and camaraderie. It was the best $3,000 investment we ever made.

October 8, 2014

League of Women Voters, Meet the Candidates, Oxford

Time just flew by. By the day of our first candidates' night event, in Oxford sponsored by the League of Women Voters, we only had a month left to go in the campaign. To be honest, I felt like the finish line got further and further away as each day passed in a blur. It felt like an eternity, each moment, grinding it out. All at the same time, the blur of meetings and classes and students and citizens and canvassing and phone banking and call time, especially, left me completely exhausted, even though I felt fit and strong. I slept okay, but I didn't go to bed until after midnight and woke up each morning by 5:30 am, if not before. The dogs kept me moving every day, and Chris had to get up early to go to work and this turned out to be the only time we saw each other during the week. So we had very little time together each day. But the whole thing made me sad, that is the time away from her and the hectic schedule with absolutely no time to myself for reflection or family, except for my short walk with the dogs each day. And I had to work my tail off to keep up with my classes and other commitments at school. Just grueling. As always, I showed up, did my best, and tried to make progress every day. But I felt robbed by the enormous demands that I put on myself and that others put on me. In 21st century campaigns, I'm not sure there is any way around this morass. I waded into it each day and counted the days to November 4. The League of Women Voters didn't care anything about how I felt. They just wanted me to show up.

The League's format invited each candidate to give an opening 2-minute speech. Then, audience members would ask their own questions of the candidates with a 90 second limit on responses. If both candidates in a race appeared, each would have a chance to respond. In my case, like every other event up to now and throughout the final month, Boehner got invited and never showed up. The first point I made at each of these events was that I had shown up, and Boehner hadn't and never would. He had important business to attend to, sure, but never appearing in the district didn't seem very respectful of the citizens of District 8. Of course, an incumbent has nothing to gain by doing the right thing, like showing up. For all of his experience and know-how, I felt like I could have scored my fair share of blows in a face-to-face conversation. But I never had the chance. We never thought we would get the opportunity to meet with Boehner, engage him in public. And he made good on that assumption. Too bad.

I'll remember three very distinct things about tonight's event for as long as I live. First, Larry and Burt came in together just a few minutes before the start time, and sat down in the back. They never said a word to me before or afterward. They never looked at me, never clapped or responded or supported me in any way, shape, or form. They continued to punish me in public and they should have been my supporters. Shame on them. Second, hardly anyone came to the event. Maybe 20 people came, not even coming close to filling the room. The emptiness of the room just fed the beast of indifference that clouded so much of this campaign season. No one really seemed to care. And third, one of my supporters got up to ask me a question and went on a rampage against Boehner. The moderator had to ask her to refrain from partisan attacks. She wouldn't stop. The moderator asked her to sit down and stop her question. She wouldn't stop. Finally, I had to intervene by cutting her off, and saying, "I think there was a question in there somewhere, Marie, about jobs in the region. Just let me take a crack at that one, okay?" And then I made a response and she sat down.

We didn't win any votes tonight. Boehner didn't show up. People who should have been my friends treated me like a pariah. Wildly supportive supporters didn't really do me any good.

But I got sharper, and sharper each step of the way.

MIAMI
UNIVERSITY
HAMILTON EVENT,
MEET THE
CANDIDATES

We continued with call time, and Gerald and I kept making money. Some of our days started to drag, though, as the election got closer and donors felt more and more "tapped out," as they liked to describe their current status as money givers to campaigns. But we still made headway, and we continued to call people back to give again, which many people did, and we continued to chase people we had called many times and couldn't get to commit. We did nab some of these donors, and they were very special calls.

Dial. Ring, ring, ring … Answer.

"Hello?"

"Hi, Jerry, this is Tom Poetter calling again from District 8. Our own poll puts us just eight points behind Boehner, and we are making great progress. We know he is polling and spending millions on TV. Will you please help us finance our final media push?"

"Sure, how does $250 sound?"

"Great, Gerald is sitting right here and he'll take your credit card information. Thank you, Jerry, for coming through and for making a difference in our campaign."

Then I would walk away, handing the phone to Gerald, pumping my fists like I'd just made the winning basket in a championship game. Sometimes Katarina saw this happen and just marveled at how into it I had gotten considering that I had sworn off campaigns, claimed I hated every minute of it, and said that call time, at some point, would kill me. All true, but my competitive side won out sometimes, and I have to admit that it really felt sweet sometimes to win on the phone.

Tonight we had been invited to Miami's Hamilton Campus downtown hub for a "Meet the Candidates" night, somewhat hastily thrown together just a week out. We agreed to go because I knew the organizer well and thought the Hamilton press exposure would be great, but we had no idea who would show up or what the format would be like. We tried to get details, but at this point, I could do just about anything anyone wanted me to do. It really didn't matter. Stand on my head? No problem. Whistle "Dixie"? Absolutely. Give a two-minute opening off the cuff? Yes. Answer questions about Ebola and Legalizing Marijuana and Sequestration and the Highway Bill? Sure ... I didn't need notes, or preparation at this point. I studied, practiced answers, spoke and spoke and spoke. I had it down, and began enjoying events more and more.

Tonight, the most beautiful things happened. When we arrived, the greeters treated us all like royalty. The food turned out to be excellent, and we ate a lot! And the conveners packed the place with students and citizens eager to hear the candidates. They packed the room with over 75 people and the media showed up to interview everyone. The candidates who showed up had become friends, and I especially liked listening to Suzi Rubin from Monroe and Rick Smith, who was running for a statehouse seat in neighboring Warren County but who also wanted the exposure from the event and the practice, no doubt. He turned out to be one of the best, most genuine, funny and entertaining and smart candidates I met on the trail all season. He didn't have the polish or the flair of the statewide candidates, but practice had really improved his game.

I got into it, perhaps a little over excited on several answers, and in one impassioned plea asked the crowd how we could go on treating our educational system, especially our teachers and students, the way we had since the passing of No Child Left Behind. It was one of the few moments on the campaign trail during the entire eight months of fury that a crowd liked my ideas about education and listened to me. Perhaps it was because we presented tonight in a setting associated with higher education, I don't know, but it felt right and I made a dent in my own journey. I should have been able to make more progress with an educational agenda, but it really didn't play very well to voters. But tonight, it sang.

When we walked out tonight, I felt like we had earned 75 new votes. How could anyone in attendance at a packed house event even consider voting for Boehner after hearing me speak in public? I felt that way all the way home and then collapsing into bed that night; I fell asleep smiling.

October 22, 2014

CANDIDATE FORUM, MEET THE CANDIDATES, TROY

Remember, not showing up at the Troy Forum in April may have cost us Miami County in the primary. I wasn't about to make the same mistake twice. We showed up at the big event in Troy way ahead of time, with plenty of wiggle room to eat and prep a little for the event in the car. This would be the last big, scheduled event of the campaign, except for our "victory party" on election night. Our time would be spent almost solely on voter contact through election day.

We rolled into Troy with all the confidence in the world. Of course, Boehner wouldn't show up. All we had to worry about were the audience and the questions. I hadn't really gotten a zinger yet; I could handle most questions fairly well by now. Miami County citizens packed the meeting room. That was nice to see, with political electricity filling the air.

And tonight, I met an even wider array of candidates from across the region, for state house, for state senate, for commissioner, for municipal judge, for state school board, etc. Of course, some of my old favorites would show, like Dee Gillis, running for state senate in a brutal mash up with Republican incumbent Bill Beagle. They ultimately had a tremendously negative showdown tonight, the culmination of a months-long ruckus that had been playing out in campaign ads on TV. I hadn't seen a local race get quite this nasty in our region before, but the race marked the nexus of a supermajority for the Republicans, and they would leave no stone unturned

212

to keep that vote in place, come hell or high water. I felt a little sorry for Dee having to face all of that, but she handled it well and fought back tooth and nail. She never withered.

After we gave our opening statements, I caught the eye of a teenaged high school student in the front row. When our eyes met, he mouthed these words to me:

"You can't win."

I mouthed back, "I know that," and smiled and shrugged my shoulders at him. He thought this would really hurt me, I think, but he wasn't saying anything I didn't already know. I laughed inside, his audacity made me relax and I just let it rip.

The rotation of questions, with so many candidates on the dais, proved to be long. I got four questions the entire night over a 90-minute session, but since I was the only federal candidate, the moderator asked me all the "big" questions. With the Ebola Virus scare taking shape in the news, she asked, "Mr. Poetter, as a member of congress, what would you do to stem the spread of the Ebola Virus?"

I moved the microphone in front of me and asked her and the audience, "In 90 seconds? Solve the Ebola Crisis, seriously?" The crowd roared, laughing, they knew it was an impossible question. But I turned it my way.

"Look, we have a medical doctor on the panel tonight who already admitted that we don't know enough about what is happening with the virus to know exactly what to do to stop its spread. But we do know one thing for sure. We know that the Center for Disease Control has suffered budget cuts that have crippled it. We need to get to the root of the problem with critical national services: If we don't fund them right, they won't serve us well. I believe the CDC will come through, and this threat will be contained ultimately. But we have to look deeper, making sure that we are doing our due diligence to protect the American people. Sequestration isn't protecting anyone, and as in this case, it's only hurting us."

I got a nice round of applause for that answer, and I got the same kind of softball tossed at me by the moderator next round, "Mr. Poetter, what would you do about legalizing Marijuana?"

"Really? 90 seconds on Ebola and 90 seconds on Marijuana? I should have gone to medical school!" The crowd liked that one too, especially with the tension over Beagle and Gillis mounting each round, as they tried to claim they hadn't gone "negative" while slinging mud at each other the entire night on stage. I talked for a minute about the changing nature of society, and that while I hadn't made up my mind yet about legalizing marijuana, that we really needed to study the scenario playing out in legalized Colorado, for instance, but ultimately that the "War on Drugs" had crippled so many, been ineffective, and demonized marijuana, criminalizing its use in a way that may not be defensible in this day and age. Time would tell. Etc., etc.

We all made our closing statements, and I went off the board, not reading my prepared closing. It felt good, and natural, and clean to just say my last two cents worth in public. I'm glad I had that opportunity, and that I looked up from my notes tonight.

When the moderator adjourned the meeting, all of the candidates stood to shake hands, but Bill Beagle, sitting next to me all night, stayed seated with me, and turned to me, reached for my hand to shake it, and said, "Nice job tonight."

I shook his hand, "You, too. Nice to meet you, too. Of course, I'm rooting for Dee, but you won't hold that against me, right?"

"No," he laughed, "I just want this to be over."

"Me, too," I said, "It's killing me, I'm so tired, and I'm so happy that there are only two weeks to go."

He agreed, "Campaigns are murder. Good luck to you, Tom."

"Good luck, Bill."

I felt in that moment like we were replaying the end of the Looney Tunes Cartoon where Ralph the Wolf and Sam the Sheepdog say good night after a long day at work. It's not personal, after all, none of it. It's about the work, since we're all on the same side, running on the same wheel in the same cycle.

Beagle crushed Gillis in the general election.

Maybe in another time warp Bill Beagle and I could have been friends, the kind of friends like Mondale and Dole, friends personally, but carrying around grossly different ideological and practical baggage, searching for a middle way. But that wouldn't happen. Troy faded into our memory banks quickly. It's hard to claim a win by forfeit when your opponent doesn't show up. That's old news. I can just imagine how opposite our responses would have been to Ebola and Marijuana. I would have liked to have the chance to draw some distinctions. I think I could do that in 90 seconds!

At the end of the night, if I had faced a real opponent, maybe I could have said, "Nice job, John," and shook his hand. And he could have said, "Nice job, Tom. See you at the polls."

Wouldn't that have been nice? A dream come true? I wish that's how democracy worked. But I never got the perfect ending to a Looney Tunes cartoon. Only a dream.

October 23, 2014

QUITTING CALL TIME

This chapter is a tribute to Katarina Vicar, the greatest campaign manager of all time. She loves call time more than anything, and more than anyone I've ever known or will ever know.

Katarina and I had our problems. Sometimes we argued; of course, we both can be bullheaded. Yet, I saw her clearly, and appreciated her very, very much. She devoted herself completely to the race, and made it her number one job to get as much as she could out of me, despite my reservations and my limitations. Her goal: To mount the most effective race against Boehner in his entire political career, and to put him out of business if at all possible. She couldn't do it without me getting better, and investing myself completely in the race. And I had to learn to do call time, and raise money. To her, this was the most important thing, and everything else would fall into place. She won. I got better, and did my job.

She put together a really sharp, effective mailing campaign with The Jackson Team. Eight mass mailings went out to hundreds of thousands of voters over the course of the last 10 weeks of the campaign. People all over the region had gotten my mail and commented on the pieces, remarking how awesome they were and how glad they were to be on our mailing lists. She did all of it.

Katarina did what she had to do at times, making tough calls—including making sure that Bill didn't come back to the campaign after quitting—and taking over call time. Bill wanted to come back after Katarina joined us, after

215

Bill heard about our growth and momentum, but she nixed that. They never could have gotten along. I missed Marv on the campaign, but I came to terms with the fact that Katarina and he couldn't co-exist. The fact will always remain that I needed a campaign manager who knew what to do and who could devote the time and energy necessary to doing it right. I got that with Katarina, though it cost me some people along the way, some I may never even know about. But I think that would be the case in almost any situation. I have no regrets. Choosing Katarina was the right and best choice for the campaign, and for me.

Katarina put a field campaign in place to beat Guyette in the primary, and then she hired Jack and Lynn and Gerald to bring us home in the general election. We needed all of their expertise in running our field operations, and they worked together very well. Katarina didn't like the idea of the interns, originally, but once she saw what they could do, she was all in. That's a great quality to have, admitting that you might have been wrong and letting others have the spotlight for getting it right. She didn't like it, but she didn't stand in Jack's way, either. We all won by putting the interns to work.

Katarina pushed the poll, the AMA with Reddit, the many personal appearances I made, the quality of my speeches and the quality of my thinking about politics and the campaign. She taught me how real campaigns are run. She taught me how to put myself fully out there.

As much as I hated to admit it at times, since I wanted to be in charge, I needed her to guide me and jerk me around at times. Candidates need campaign managers. It's a tough dance, and no one really wins, except the people who get to see and hear a polished, strong candidate in the end, who stands for something and can at least give a 90 second speech. I could do all of that as a result of my interaction with her, my learning from her.

And she taught me how to make money on the phone.

I told Katarina that I would know when I was finished raising money, and that once I knew it, I would stop complaining about call time, and just quit. I wouldn't quit if we didn't have enough money to finish the job. I would only quit when we had enough money and call time didn't yield.

The day after our great showing at the Troy Candidates' Night, Gerald and I settled in for our daily three hours of call time. The phones hadn't yielded much the past few days. We had plenty of numbers to call, but donors had begun shutting off the spigots. It just didn't feel like any new money would be possible to find, and that old money had come through for us all ready so many times. We hit roadblocks this week on the phone, and today, it got worse. After about 50 calls, with everyone telling me it was too late for money to make any difference, and that I shouldn't be on the phone at all, that I should be knocking on people's doors or calling them on the phone to vote for me, I decided they were right.

I looked at Gerald after one last terrible call, and said, "That's it. That's my last fundraising call."

I stood up, and shook Gerald's hand, and said, "You did a great job the past six weeks, Gerald. I'm so glad we got to do this part of the campaign together. It was really fun. But it's over. I'm going to tell Katarina." He shook my hand and said, "Good luck with that, Tom."

We both laughed as I walked down the hall to Katarina's office.

I knocked on her door like I had done a million times, and poked my head in. I said, "Hey, just wanted you to know that I made my last fundraising call. You need to get cracking on how you are going to use me for those hours now."

I started to walk back down the hallway, but knew that she would yell once the initial shock wore off, "Poetter, get back in here. You're not quitting call time!"

I went back in, of course. During our last conversation about call time over the next few minutes, I just stated the obvious. I should be calling voters, not donors, now. I should be knocking on doors. And the money just isn't there. We had enough money raised to make it to the end. But the dream of raising enough for TV, and having the production time to get them to air, just wasn't going to happen. We came close, but didn't make it. It wasn't her fault; we just got started too late. Look at all the progress we made, and the campaign we put together. Amazing.

Me stating these things really helped her and made her feel better. In a very generous act, she released me. I went to lunch, and never looked back.

I hated call time. I hated asking strangers and friends, both, for money. Sometimes it energized, but most times it deflated. In the end, Katarina really wanted to make it to $200,000 raised. We came up just short, raising almost $195 K. Remarkable, really, for a short, 8-month campaign. Giving up call time gave me back three hours a day of my life. I really, really hated call time, and didn't miss it.

Goodbye call time, and good riddance. But thanks, Katarina, for teaching me how to do it, and for showing me how to become a real candidate, and for running a real campaign.

October 30, 2014

HAMILTON CANVASS WITH DEL, HALLOWEEN CENTRAL

Because my remaining time on the campaign now focused on canvassing and phone banking, we pushed as hard as we could as a team to knock on as many doors and to call as many prospective voters as possible in the days remaining before the election. Headquarters buzzed each night with callers manning phone banks. We made thousands of calls each day. I got myself into the cycle as well, especially at the end, trying to make at least 150 calls a day (2–4 hours of calling). I wound up talking to 20 or 25 voters each cycle. Many of them acted disinterested. This was heartbreaking at times. At the end of tough calls, I often said to the voter, "I'm a candidate for federal office, and I'm calling you on the phone myself. Boehner isn't calling you or coming to your door. Ask me anything you want." Oftentimes the citizen just said, "I'll vote my conscience at the polls. Goodbye." No discussion, nothing; even Democrats said this to me. Weird.

In this part of the country, maybe everywhere, many citizens just want to be left alone by politicians. Many don't want to participate in the political process or talk politics. I sometimes got fed up with politics, too. But many people do harbor indifference, if not a complete disinterest in the enterprise. I'm not sure what we can do to reverse this, much of it may be cultural and in fact, perhaps, intractable. But I'm hopeful that the more people call and answer and talk, on the phone, at the doors, and at the polls, then the more experience we all have with responding to each other, debating ideas, and coming up with ways forward that are just and equitable. I keep having this hope against all hope.

Tonight I would be walking in Hamilton with Del, one of our interns who had been walking a lot with me lately. What a great, impressive figure Del cut, about 6' and handsome, and smart, funny, helpful, interning. Tonight, the night before Halloween, we would see things we could never forget. We tried to knock on about 50 doors before sunset, getting started after phone banking at around the dinner hour, 5 pm.

The first person that broke the mold was Mr. Turner. He answered the door at dinnertime dressed only in a speedo swimsuit. Standing about 5'10" tall and weighing well over 350 lbs, I never saw a person this big with so little on. He stood in the doorway, completely nonplussed, asking us questions and grilling us and then ultimately telling us we had won his vote. What a great time. It's safe to say that neither of us had ever met anyone like him, or had seen anyone like him, especially in that condition.

As we walked down the street, I stopped in the middle of the sidewalk and we faced each other, far enough out of earshot of Mr. Turner's door.

"Have you ever seen or met anyone like that in your entire life?"

Del answered, "No, Sir. I can't say that I have," and we laughed.

"Me, either, but I have the feeling things have just started to get crazy."

Before we got to the next house, a man using his water hose on his plants in the front yard across the street waved us over, and we went to talk to him even though his door wasn't on our list to knock on. Throughout the campaign, I made it a rule to always hand my literature to anyone who was out that we saw. I didn't want to be a mystery to people and if someone was out and not running from us, they might vote for me if they met me. I have to say that over the entire campaign I never had one bad experience doing this.

When we got to him he turned off the hose, asked us what we were doing, looked at our literature, and launched into a long harangue about the evils of the ACA, how he knew people who had gotten caught in the health shuffle, several fantastic stories about people he knew who couldn't get organ transplants, and such and such and so on. We just couldn't get away from him. What a spirited distraction he turned out to be, maybe even working for the other side, undermining us. I tried to walk away, and he'd say one more thing, fantastic, and bombastic, and we had to rebut. It had actually started to turn to dusk, and we still had a lot of doors to knock on.

Finally, I said, "Mr. Burns, it's been great meeting you, but we still have 15 doors left to visit. Good night." And he yelled after us, but I told Del, "Don't turn around, just keep walking."

As we moved toward the intersection, we stopped at the corner, now out of earshot of the distractor. I said, "Wow, that guy was so hard to get away from. Was he serious? Could any or all of that be anything close to true?"

Del couldn't answer, flabbergasted and tired. Instead, he said, "I think our next door is right across the street."

But before I had a chance to answer, with the moon rising on the horizon, and dusk turning to night, a young man with no shirt on and a bandana covering his head drove a go cart at top speed, maybe 40 mph, right past us on the street and through the intersection. He yelped out something as he sped by, unintelligible, and his confederate flag, blowing in the wind and dangling from a red fiberglass pole on the back of the kart, stunned us into complete and total silence. We just stood there with our jaws touching the ground.

Finally, after a few moments watching him race up the street, screech to a halt and turn around, he made a return pass right in front of us going the other way. I turned to Del and said, "Now I've seen everything. I think that's it for me tonight. This is crazy."

"Wow," Del said, "that just happened."

"Yes, it did. Let's get a hamburger."

I fed Del on the way home, and we laughed and hooted about every single crazy thing we saw that night. How could it all have happened all at once to us?

We marveled at the beautiful half moon glowing in the night sky as we drove back to Oxford. The world was at least half crazy; nature can't explain everything.

November 4, 2014

ELECTION DAY

I learned from Katarina that it's a campaign tradition for the candidate to work right up until the time the polls close. No way a candidate can live with leaving even one vote on the table. Get everyone humanly possible to the polls, don't quit while there's still time left in the race, leave nothing to chance. So I walked all day.

I think Katarina and Jack drank all day. I can't blame them!

But I walked the entire day in Middletown. Gerald went with me, and by 4 pm I had reached my limit. So few people were home. It rained the whole time, making it difficult to walk and mark our sheets and stay somewhat dry. Miserable.

We had lunch late on the road, and knocked on a few more doors, and I quit. I drove Gerald home and I went to my house to prep for the victory party. I felt nervous, but I didn't really know what to think, or how to act. I just worked in the house, got food ready, waited for Chris to come home, and opened a beer to share with her when she came in. In those few moments before she arrived, alone in the house, I felt completely at ease, at peace with the entire situation. I thought, "It's okay, no matter what happens. It's over." Chris felt excited, like I did, and we talked and reminisced about all that had happened, then the boys came home, Mitch and Sam congratulating me, and asking me how relieved I was for it all to finally be over. I loved them so much, and hugged them, and waited for the staff, the interns, and a few special guests to arrive.

I had been telling Katarina that I wanted everyone out at 10 pm. We would know the score by then, and I was too tired to engage in a long, drawn out party. Let's celebrate and be done with it. She reluctantly agreed, but this option made sense for Chris and the boys and me and would be much cheaper! Friends brought food, I bought pizza, and by 9:30 pm, which came very quickly, the house had gotten packed with people.

I felt so honored to have everyone who worked on the campaign at the house. I wanted them all to know how much I appreciated their efforts. We ate and drank and talked and laughed. Very fun.

Finally, the results trickled in and then all of a sudden a burst of precincts popped in each county, giving a snapshot of the final score, which turned out to be Boehner 67, Poetter 27, and Condit 6. Over 50,000 people voted for me, but Boehner creamed us. And we started to see that almost every Democrat in the state suffered the same fate, beginning with the disastrous Governor race and on down the line. A complete and total wipeout. Perhaps pundits saw it coming, but the Republican landslide of 2014 had a direct impact on us. The results were real. We lost big. Most polling couldn't have predicted this level of political bloodbath.

The score really hurt Katarina, who had tears in her eyes. But I bucked up and gave a thank you speech to the group. It was heartfelt, not eloquent. I wanted everyone to know that the most important thing I felt in my heart was gratitude for the incredible effort they put forth, and the support the room gave me all the way through the race. Everyone clapped, then I said, "Now everyone out. Go out and enjoy your lives, and have a great day tomorrow."

I pushed everyone out the door, and no one balked, except Katarina.

Katarina remained crushed that no one from Boehner's camp called. She had tried to get a phone number all week from his people but got stonewalled at every turn.

As a result, I conceded on Facebook at around midnight after everyone went to bed and all the excitement had died down. Awful, no class, sad, that we couldn't concede for real. I didn't really care, but I knew Katarina cared. Campaigns like ours are supposed to end with a cordial concession call. I never got to make it.

But I'm the one who got my ass kicked, so any talk about custom and respect is merely sour grapes. To be honest, I never slept better in my whole life.

November 5, 2014

POST MORTEM

The newspapers all called and I gave a few quotes on Wednesday after the election. For a few days, the papers recounted the races and said goodbye to all the losers and hello again to all the winners.

I felt a huge sense of relief, but put my head down, working with the staff to clear out of the office space and to get the last details of the campaign, especially the finances, sorted out with the staff and the treasurer.

We had financial reports to make soon, and we had to have everything in order so we could formally close the campaign. This actually took several months to do before it was all officially over and the campaign closed.

Katarina and I met only one more time before she moved back home. We parted amicably, but it was all so sad for it to be over for her. She wanted to keep going. I wanted to go back to my life.

I met a very nice response from all kinds of people in the weeks after the election who praised me for running and thought I had done a good job, and said they thought that I had actually made a pretty decent showing considering the competition and the fact that every Democrat did poorly. I thanked them, and enjoyed the soft plunge back to earth that friends and supporters provided with their kind words and encouragement.

On the last day of our office lease, December 31, 2014, I went into Headquarters for the last time, gathered up the remaining rabble, took a last look around, and fondly moved my hand over the Formica countertop that Danny Sens had installed just a year before. I missed my friend, and would have traded everything to have another beer with him, and to laugh.

I turned out the lights, locked the door, and dropped the key off with the landlord.

She asked me as I handed her the key, "Will you run again?"

"Not a chance," I said, and smiled, and thanked her for the great space.

I staggered to my car, routinely buckled my belt, and started the engine, all by rote. I just sat there for a moment, thinking of all of it, at once, the entire crazy, ridiculous, wonderful year of running for congress and losing so badly. I drove home, without incident, in a mist.

I needed time to decompress, so I didn't start writing this memoir for almost six months after the election. But even that felt too soon. The fact is that memoirs don't fall from trees, so getting this book to press for the next election cycle meant that I had to get into it pretty quickly. I really appreciate you sticking with me. In the next chapter I propose how we might re-think congressional campaign funding, and add some critical facts about our race.

What We Should Do As a Nation to Make Every Race Fairer

(Note: I am presenting the following plan as my idea. If it resembles any other idea or set of ideas ever proposed by anyone else, I did not lift it from them because I haven't done extensive research on it. Therefore, it's merely accidental. If there are similarities, the adage applies: "Great minds think alike." Not plagiarism.)

First, some stats on what we accomplished in our race. My Field Director estimates that we knocked on 30,000 doors as a campaign, and made up to 90,000 phone calls to constituents in total, not including an additional 20,000 donor calls. This took an amazing amount of organization and effort in a short amount of time. Many people deserve congratulations for these efforts, up and down the line. We raised just short of $200,000. This may not seem like a lot, but most people who have been involved in campaigns like ours know that this is a tremendous achievement. I worked the phones, but Katarina and Marv and Chad put in the lion's share of the research effort, especially with potential donors.

I have often said that using my donation list is a sure way to make $200,000. Most of these folks gave to me without hesitation and generously. If we had a few more months, we could have run TV and radio ads because we would have been able to raise the money. We simply ran out of time.

All of this being said, it's obvious that this district is gerrymandered and no Democrat or progressive of any kind has any chance of winning anytime soon. And, of course, Boehner spent $17 million in the 2014 election cycle. Many called it a legacy election, with Boehner not so much interested necessarily in trouncing me but in winning by a big enough margin to insure his continued election inside the House as Speaker.

So, it's obvious that our states and our nation have created a huge problem: the system itself is rigged so heartily toward the vagaries of political culture, geography, and demographics that even "competitive" races are very difficult to achieve. Throw in the factor of money, and you have such an uneven playing field in most cases that it's a miracle that anyone who is an incumbent ever gets beaten at the polls. And the situation means that it is very difficult for citizens to run for congress or higher office of any kind. It's difficult for solid citizens to take on the powerful. Perhaps it's okay that the system is basically closed to new blood and innovation, that not everyone can do it. But if almost no one can do it, because of the time involved, the expertise needed, and the money required, then we aren't going to get a very representative body in our legislatures. We will always have what we have now: moneyed, incumbent-driven, special interest-centered gridlock. We can do better.

And remember, my point here is not necessarily to produce new winners, because voters will have to decide that. But instead, how about making it more possible to run well and to make the races more competitive from the start? True, you may argue, the parties could solve this problem themselves. Maybe, but they may be as infected as our entire system is. You read the book, right, and didn't just skip to the last chapter?

So here's my plan, it's not that hard. And I know there are problems with this plan, but hear me out. Perhaps we can commit to doing something different than what we are doing now in future election cycles. The idea is to start thinking about solutions, and the core ideas that support them. We have to start somewhere. So, for instance …

Let's cut the formal timeframe for all federal races down to 10 months. Let's make declaring a candidacy due by January 10 of the election year. No formal campaign activities should take place in the previous calendar year, including fundraising, prior to submitting the paperwork to be considered a candidate and to be included on the primary ballot. Let's make the limit for primary season fundraising, from January 10 to Primary Election Day in May (across the board the same date in each state), $100,000. Make that the limit for money raised and spent by the candidate for the primary. Of course, since we can't roll back, as of yet, Citizens United and the spending rules surrounding PACs and Super PACs, they may operate as they please under current law. But if they are caught coordinating with a candidate, or vice versa, then the PAC and the candidate get sudden death. No fines. A breach of any kind ends the campaign at any moment in time (including ex post facto), no matter who it is.

Once a candidate is chosen from each party in the Primary, then the nation and the parties subsidize each candidate's financial budget up to $250,000 (including what is raised but not spent on the Primary) for candidates for the U.S. House and $1,000,000 for the U.S. Senate (since senate races are statewide and the house districts are significantly smaller than the state). That money can be spent for campaign salaries, travel, media advertising, etc. However, no salaries may be paid to candidates or their relatives. Otherwise, any campaign cost that is currently acceptable would be acceptable.

But the candidates and their campaigns may not raise any further money after the Primary and may only spend $250,000 total on the General Election campaign. No personal money may be spent. No carryover money from past elections may be spent, only $250,000. Any money not spent on a general election campaign gets returned to the government and is not carried over by a campaign. For example, if a candidate raises $98,000 for the primary and spends $58,000 and wins, $40,000 goes toward the general election budget and the government and the parties contribute $210,000. The candidate who raises $88,000 and spends $70,000 and loses, gives all the raised money not spent to his or her national party.

Every two years there are 435 congressional races (or 870 candidates from the two parties) and 34 senate races (or 68 candidates, the senate has 100 seats, and ⅓ of them are up for election each two-year cycle). Under my plan, the total spent by the U.S. government and the parties (each national party chips in 25% of the total cost for their candidates) would be approximately $220 million for the congressional races and $68 million for the senate races. Let's round the cost up to total of $300 million for administration and enforcement costs.

That means that every two years the two major parties would contribute approximately $75 million to national elections and the U.S. government would contribute approximately $150 million. If we want to take money out of politics and give everyone running who can win a primary a fair shake, then this plan—funded by all citizens, not just the rich few—would hasten the realization of several key phenomena that would better our experience of politics:

- Cutting the time down for races and making it more affordable would make it possible for more people who could run to at least consider running because this somewhat levels the time commitment and financial playing fields.
- Less outside money inside campaigns means less outside influence on politicians, and perhaps less enticement for candidates to follow the money or special interests to the detriment of the people.

- Equal amounts of money spent means that expertise, ideas, experience, and efforts to interact with voters, not donors, would put candidates closer to the people, closer to developing new conversations and new approaches to improving our democratic republic. Less money makes winning votes more important than raising more money.

And finally, let's make six, two-year terms in congress (12 years) and two, six-year terms in the Senate (12 years) lifetime term limits. We need citizens in government who go back to their real jobs. We don't need lifetime politicians. Yes, some of them become experts and help us as they become wiser and more experienced. But others become fat cats, preying on the public and winning their own fortunes. They give public service a bad name. Fat cats won't disappear, but eliminating big money inside politics may take away the incentive for some to get involved in the first place.

I'm pretty sure no one will ever entertain making this whole thing simpler so that the more complex activities of campaigning and building consensus will win out. But I would like to see us take a commitment to building our political and social democracies more seriously, not merely helping to build candidates' own potential fortunes. Sometimes this takes radical ideas, and cost sharing! We could do this if citizens have the political will to see it through.

And by the way, I'm not saying that I could have beaten Boehner if we both only had $250,000 to spend on our campaigns. But I bet you Boehner would have come to the League Women Voters Event in Oxford in October of 2014 or the debate we challenged him to host in any venue of his choice, anywhere in the district or the nation. Now, that would have been something! We would have shown up! And everyone wins if that happens.